LANGUAGE ARTS

WILLIAM & MARY

THE CENTER FOR GIFTED EDUCATION

The 1940s: A Decade of Change

Second Edition

Student Guide

Grades 7-9

Kendall Hunt
publishing company

Cover image © 2011 Shutterstock, Inc.

Kendall Hunt
publishing company

www.kendallhunt.com
Send all inquiries to:
4050 Westmark Drive
Dubuque, IA 52004-1840
1-800-542-6657

Center for Gifted Education
College of William & Mary
PO Box 8795
Williamsburg, VA 23187-8795
757-221-2362
www.cfge.wm.edu

Funded by the Jacob K. Javits Program, United States Department of Education, under a subcontract from the Washington-Saratoga-Warren-Hamilton-Essex BOCES, Saratoga Springs, New York.

Copyright © 1998, 2011 by Center for Gifted Education

ISBN 978-0-7575-6603-5

Printed by: Lightning Source
United States of America
Batch number: 426603

Printed in the United States of America

Contents

Letter to Student

Dear Student:

You are participating in a special language arts unit called *The 1940s: A Decade of Change*. It is organized around the concept of change and has many activities designed to help you understand this concept.

A wide variety of literature will allow you to explore the concept of change. The literature will stimulate discussion, writing, listening, vocabulary study, and research activities. In class, we will read and discuss short pieces of literature, including poems and short stories. You will also read four longer works. To clarify your thinking and to help prepare for written and oral assignments, you will keep a journal. As you read the literature, you will respond to it and think critically about it by analyzing ideas, vocabulary, and structure.

The purpose of this book is to provide you with additional materials that you will need to participate in the unit. All of the unit short stories and poems are contained in this book, as well as Activity Pages related to all literature selections.

During the course of the unit, you will be using several teaching models to help organize your thinking. They include:

1. Literature Web Model
2. Vocabulary Web Model
3. Hamburger Model for Persuasive Writing
4. Writing Process Model
5. Reasoning Model
6. Research Model

Your teacher will explain how these models work and how you can use them as you read the unit literature and complete the required activities.

Sincerely,

Curriculum Development Team

Center for Gifted Education at The College of William & Mary

Glossary of Literary Terms

The following list contains a selection of literary terms which may be useful in understanding the discussion of literature within this unit.

Character: a person portrayed in an artistic piece, such as a drama or novel.

Climax: the turning point in a plot or dramatic action; a moment of great or culminating intensity in a narrative or drama, especially at the conclusion of a crisis.

Creative nonfiction: sometimes is known as literary or narrative nonfiction, takes real events and retells them, filling in details as well as possible from what is known or researched.

Denouement: the final resolution or clarification of a dramatic or narrative plot; the events following the climax of a drama or novel in which such a resolution or clarification takes place.

Foreshadowing: the hints or suggestions that an event will take place at a future time within the selection.

Irony: A literary device in which action or language stands in contrast to what appears to be true or expected.

Motivation: an inducement or incentive to action; in a story, the psychological or social factors that drive character action.

Plot: the plan of events or main story in a narrative or drama.

Setting: the time, place, and circumstances in which a narrative, drama, or film takes place.

Theme: an implicit or recurrent idea; a motif; a central idea that permeates a poem, short story, or novel.

Models

The following pages include information about some teaching models that you can use to help organize your thinking.

The Literature Web Model

The Literature Web is a model designed to guide interpretation of a literature selection by helping you to connect your personal response with elements of the text. The web may be completed independently and/or as a tool for discussion. The web has five parts:

1. *Key words:* interesting, unfamiliar, striking, or particularly important words and phrases contained within the text

2. *Feelings:* your feelings and the specific text details that inspire them; the characters' feelings; and the feelings that you infer the author intended to inspire

3. *Ideas:* major themes and main ideas of the text; key concepts

4. *Images and symbols:* notable sensory images in the text; "pictures" the text creates in your mind and the details that inspire them; symbols for abstract ideas

5. *Structure:* the formal elements of the writing and their contribution to meaning; may include such features as use of unusual time sequence in narrative, such as flashbacks, use of voice, use of figurative language, etc.; style of writing

Figure 1-1:
Literature Web Model

The Vocabulary Web Model

The Vocabulary Web is a tool for exploring a word in depth. Find the definition of the word and its part of speech, synonyms and antonyms, word stems, and origin. For word families, try to find at least three other words that use one or more of your word's stems. Then create an example to explain your word (a sentence, an analogy, a picture or diagram, etc.). Use the Vocabulary Web to organize your responses.

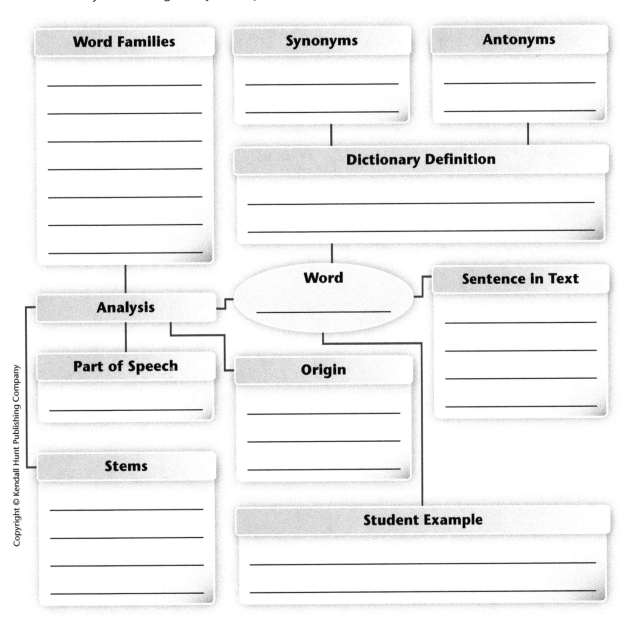

Copyright © Kendall Hunt Publishing Company

Figure 1-2:
Vocabulary Web Model

Unit vocabulary words you may want to explore include:

From "The Lottery":

interminably

paraphernalia

perfunctory

reprimand

From "One Friday Morning":

Abolitionists

arbitrarily

discriminated

feted

From *Maus II:*

genocide

Holocaust

From Soldiers' Stories:

casualties

rendezvous

barricade

inevitable

shrapnel

The Hamburger Model for Persuasive Writing

The Hamburger Model uses a sandwich as a metaphor to help you construct a paragraph or essay. Begin by stating your point of view on the issue in question (the top bun). Then provide reasons, or evidence, to support your claim; you should try to incorporate at least three supportive reasons (the "patties"). Elaboration on the reasons provides additional detail (the "fixings"). A concluding sentence or paragraph wraps up the piece of writing (the bottom bun).

Figure 1-3: Hamburger Model for Persuasive Writing

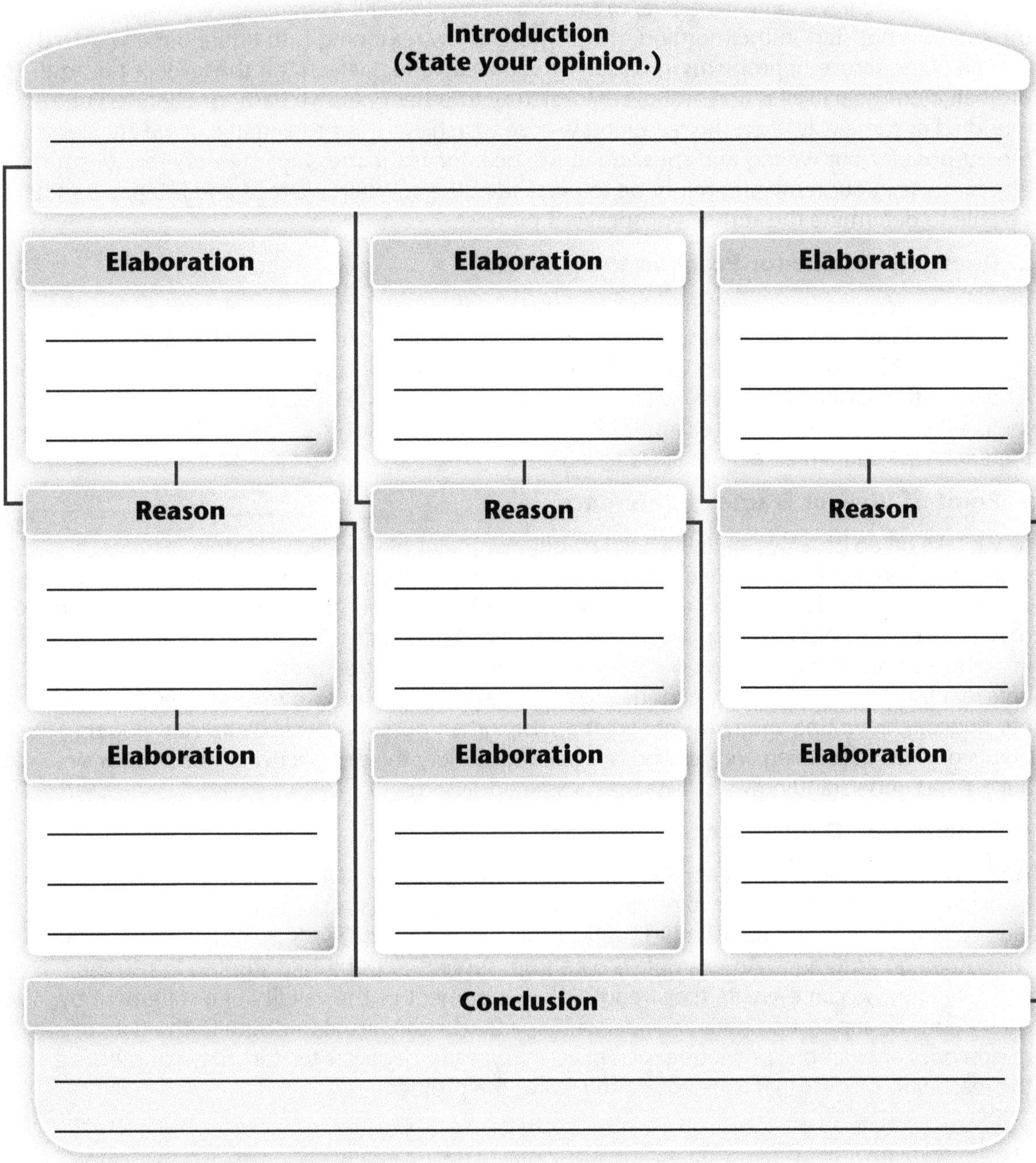

Introduction
(State your opinion.)

_____
_____

Elaboration	Elaboration	Elaboration
_____	_____	_____
_____	_____	_____
_____	_____	_____

Reason	Reason	Reason
_____	_____	_____
_____	_____	_____
_____	_____	_____

Elaboration	Elaboration	Elaboration
_____	_____	_____
_____	_____	_____
_____	_____	_____

Conclusion

_____
_____

The Reasoning Model

Paul's Elements of Reasoning (1992) is a model for critical thinking that emphasizes the following eight elements: *issue, purpose, point of view, assumptions, concepts, evidence, inferences,* and *implications or consequences.* You should use the terms and the model in approaching problems and issues.

The eight Elements of Reasoning are as follows:

1. Purpose, Goal, or End View

We reason to achieve some objective, to satisfy a desire, to fulfill some need. For example, if the car does not start in the morning, the purpose of my reasoning is to figure out a way to get to work. One source of problems in reasoning is traceable to "defects" at the level of purpose or goal. If our goal itself is unrealistic, contradictory to other goals we have, or confused or muddled in some way, then the reasoning we use to achieve it is problematic. If we are clear on the purpose for our writing and speaking, it will help focus the message in a coherent direction. The purpose in our reasoning might be to persuade others. When we read and listen, we should be able to determine the author's or speaker's purpose.

2. Question at Issue (or Problem to Be Solved)

When we attempt to reason something out, there is at least one question at issue or problem to be solved (if not, there is no reasoning required). If we are not clear about what the question or problem is, it is unlikely that we will find a reasonable answer, or one that will serve our purpose. As part of the reasoning process, we should be able to formulate the question to be answered or the issue to be addressed. For example, "Why won't the car start?" or "Should libraries censor materials that contain objectionable language?"

3. Point of View or Frame of Reference

As we take on an issue, we are influenced by our own point of view. For example, parents of young children and librarians might have different points of view on censorship issues. The price of a shirt may seem low to one person while it seems high to another because of a different frame of reference. Any defect in our point of view or frame of reference is a possible source of problems in our reasoning. Our point of view may be too narrow, may not be precise enough, may be unfairly biased, and so forth. By considering multiple points of view, we may sharpen or broaden our thinking. In writing and speaking, we may strengthen our arguments by acknowledging other points of view. In listening and reading, we need to identify the perspective of the speaker or author and understand how it affects the message delivered.

4. Experiences, Data, Evidence

When we reason, we must be able to support our point of view with reasons or evidence. Evidence is important in order to distinguish opinions from reasons or to create a reasoned judgment. Evidence and data should support the author's or speaker's point of view and can strengthen an argument. An example is data from surveys or published studies. In reading and listening, we can evaluate the strength of an argument or the validity of a statement by examining the supporting data or evidence. Experiences can also contribute to the data of our reasoning. For example, previous experiences in trying to get a car to start may contribute to the reasoning process that is necessary to resolve the problem.

Adapted from Paul, R. (1992). Critical thinking: What every person needs to survive in a rapidly changing world. CA: Foundation for Critical Thinking.

5. Concepts and Ideas

Reasoning requires the understanding and use of concepts and ideas (including definitional terms, principles, rules, or theories). When we read and listen, we can ask ourselves, "What are the key ideas presented?" When we write and speak, we can examine and organize our thoughts around the substance of concepts and ideas. Some examples of concepts are freedom, friendship, and responsibility.

6. Assumptions

We need to take some things for granted when we reason. We need to be aware of the assumptions we have made and the assumptions of others. If we make faulty assumptions, this can lead to defects in reasoning. As a writer or speaker we make assumptions about our audience and our message. For example, we might assume that others will share our point of view; or we might assume that the audience is familiar with the First Amendment when we refer to "First Amendment rights." As a reader or listener we should be able to identify the assumptions of the writer or speaker.

7. Inferences

Reasoning proceeds by steps called inferences. An inference is a small step of the mind, in which a person concludes that something is so because of something else being so or seeming to be so. The tentative conclusions (inferences) we make depend on what we assume as we attempt to make sense of what is going on around us. For example, we see dark clouds and infer that it is going to rain; or we know the movie starts at 7:00; it is now 6:45; it takes 30 minutes to get to the theater; so we cannot get there on time. Many of our inferences are justified and reasonable, but many are not. We need to distinguish between the raw data of our experiences and our interpretations of those experiences (inferences). Also, the inferences we make are heavily influenced by our point of view and our assumptions.

8. Implications and Consequences

When our reasoning takes us in a certain direction, we need to look at the implications of following that line of reasoning. When we argue and support a certain point of view, for example, solid reasoning requires that we consider what the consequences might be of taking the course that we support. When we read or listen to an argument, we need to ask ourselves what follows from that way of thinking. We can also consider consequences of actions that characters in stories take, just as we can consider consequences of our own actions. For example, if I don't do my homework, I will have to stay after school to do it; if I water the lawn, it will not wither in the summer heat.

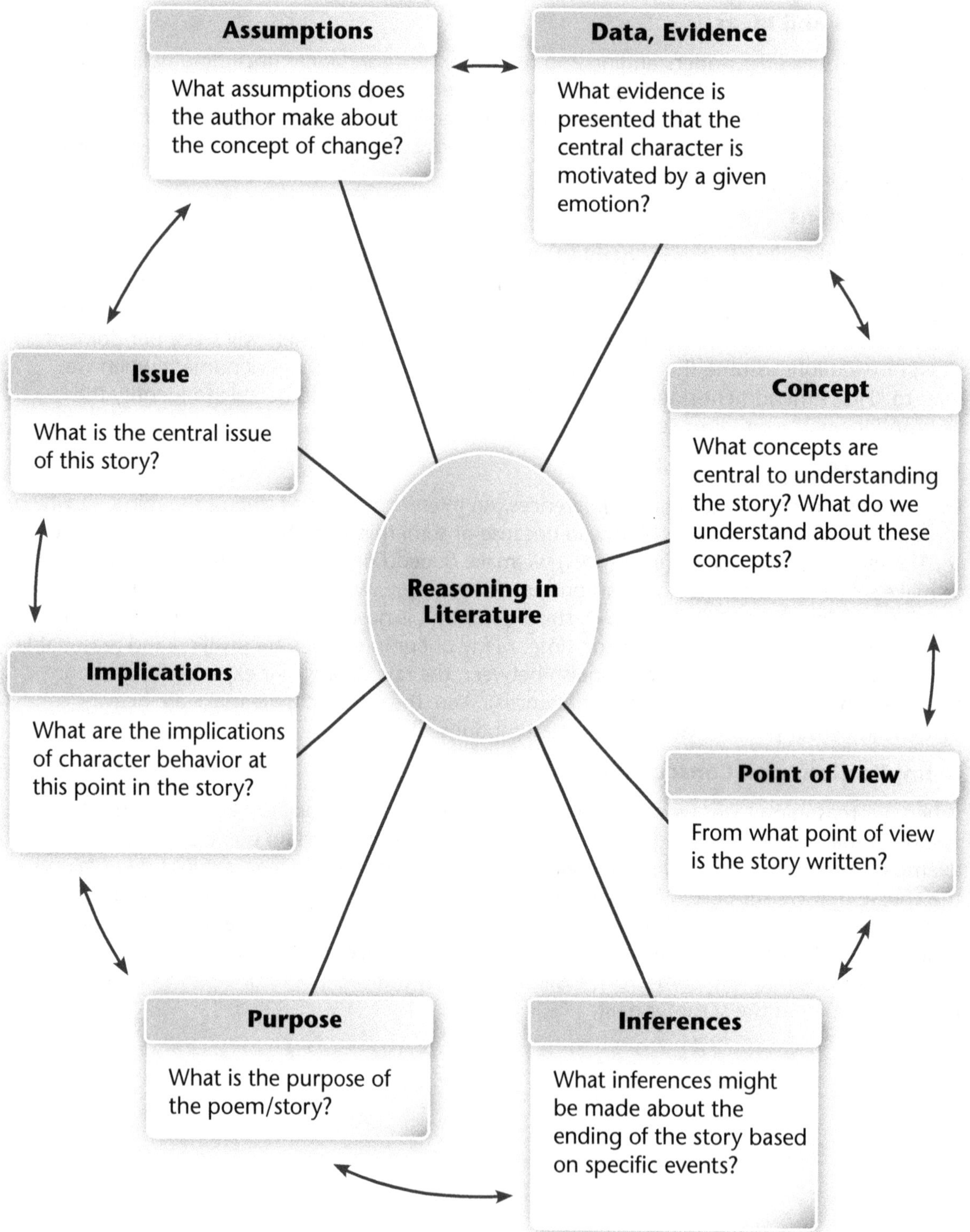

Assumptions

What assumptions does the author make about the concept of change?

Data, Evidence

What evidence is presented that the central character is motivated by a given emotion?

Issue

What is the central issue of this story?

Concept

What concepts are central to understanding the story? What do we understand about these concepts?

Implications

What are the implications of character behavior at this point in the story?

Reasoning in Literature

Point of View

From what point of view is the story written?

Purpose

What is the purpose of the poem/story?

Inferences

What inferences might be made about the ending of the story based on specific events?

Figure 1-4: Wheel of Reasoning

The 1940s: A Decade of Change · Models

The Writing Process Model

The Writing Process describes the stages that writers use to develop a written composition. The stages are not separate parts that writers go through from one to five; rather, writers move back and forth among the stages and use them to construct, clarify, and polish their writing. The Writing Process Model is used throughout the unit to help you improve your own writing.

The following are the stages of the writing process:

1. *Prewriting:* List your ideas and begin to organize them. You may want to use a graphic organizer such as a web or a Venn diagram. Graphic organizers help you to "see" what you will write about. As you write, you can add to your diagram or change it.

2. *Drafting:* Write a rough draft, getting your ideas onto paper and not worrying about mechanics such as spelling, grammar, or punctuation. Some writers call this stage "composing." Sometimes the first draft is a "messing around" stage in which your drafting or composing helps you to "hear" what you want to say.

3. *Revising:* Conferencing is an essential step in the revising stage. Ask people (friends, family, teachers) to read and listen to your work and to tell you what they like, what they'd like to know more about, and what they don't understand. This is the place to make major changes in your "composition" or draft. Sometimes you may want to go back to the prewriting stage and redo your organizer so that your paper has a new structure.

4. *Editing:* After you have revised your paper, look for the small changes that will make a big difference. Check your choice of words and identify mechanical errors. After you make the changes and corrections, proofread your work one final time. You may want to ask a friend or an adult for help.

5. *Sharing or publishing:* There are numerous ways to share and to publish your work. You can bind it into a book, post it on a blog, or submit it to a writing contest.

The Research Model

The Research Model gives you a way to approach an issue of significance and explore it. Its organization is based on the major elements of the Reasoning Model.

1. **Identify your issue or problem.**

   - What is the issue or problem?

   - Who are the stakeholders and what are their positions?

   - What is *my* position on this issue?

2. **Read about your issue and identify points of view or arguments through information sources.**

   - What are my print sources?

   - What are my media sources?

   - What are my people sources?

   - What primary and secondary source documents might I use?

   - What are my preliminary findings based on a review of existing sources?

3. **Form a set of questions that can be answered by a specific set of data.**

   - What would be the results of _____?

   - Who would benefit and by how much?

   - Who would be harmed and by how much?

   - My research questions: _____

4. **Gather evidence through research techniques such as surveys, interviews, or analysis of primary and secondary source documents.**

   - What survey questions should I ask?

   - What interview questions should I ask?

   - What generalizations do secondary sources give?

   - What data and evidence can I find in primary sources to support different sides of the issue?

5. **Manipulate and transform data so that they can be interpreted.**

   - How can I summarize what I learned?

   - Should I develop charts, diagrams, or graphs to represent my data?

6. **Draw conclusions and make inferences.**

- What do the data mean? How can I interpret what I found out?
- How do the data support my original point of view?
- How do they support other points of view?
- What conclusions can I make about the issue?
- What is my point of view now, based on the data?

7. **Determine implications and consequences.**

- What are the consequences of following the point of view that I support?
- Do I know enough or are there now new questions to be answered?

8. **Communicate your findings. (Prepare an oral presentation for classmates based on notes and written report.)**

- What are my purpose, issue, and point of view, and how will I explain them?
- What data will I use to support my point of view?
- How will I conclude my presentation?

The Lottery

Shirley Jackson

The morning of June 27th was clear and sunny, with the fresh warmth of a full-summer day; the flowers were blossoming profusely and the grass was richly green. The people of the village began to gather in the square, between the post office and the bank, around ten o'clock; in some towns there were so many people that the lottery took two days and had to be started on June 26th, but in this village, where there were only about three hundred people, the whole lottery took less than two hours, so it could begin at ten o'clock in the morning and still be through in time to allow the villagers to get home for noon dinner.

The children assembled first, of course. School was recently over for the summer, and the feeling of liberty sat uneasily on most of them; they tended to gather together quietly for a while before they broke into boisterous play, and their talk was still of the classroom and the teacher, of books and reprimands. Bobby Martin had already stuffed his pockets full of stones, and the other boys soon followed his example, selecting the smoothest and roundest stones; Bobby and Harry Jones and Dickie Delacroix— the villagers pronounced his name "Dellacroy"— eventually made a great pile of stones in one corner of the square and guarded it against the raids of the other boys. The girls stood aside, talking among themselves, looking over their shoulders at the boys, and the very small children rolled in the dust or clung to the hands of their older brothers or sisters.

Soon the men began to gather, surveying their own children, speaking of planting and rain, tractors and taxes. They stood together, away from the pile of stones in the corner, and their jokes were quiet and they smiled rather than laughed. The women, wearing faded house dresses and sweaters, came shortly after their menfolk. They greeted one another and exchanged bits of gossip as they went to join their husbands. Soon the women, standing by their husbands, began to call to their children, and the children came reluctantly, having to be called four or five times. Bobby Martin ducked under his mother's grasping hand and ran, laughing, back to the pile of stones. His father spoke up sharply, and Bobby came quickly and took his place between his father and his oldest brother.

The lottery was conducted—as were the square dances, the teen-age club, the Halloween program—by Mr. Summers, who had time and energy to devote to civic activities. He was a round-faced, jovial man and he ran the coal business, and people were sorry for him, because he had no children and his wife was a scold. When he arrived in the square, carrying the black wooden box, there was a murmur of conversation among the villagers, and he waved and called, "Little late today, folks." The post-master, Mr. Graves, followed him, carrying a three-legged stool, and the stool was put in the center of the square and Mr. Summers set the black box down on it. The villagers kept their distance, leaving a space between themselves and the stool, and when Mr. Summers said, "Some of you fellows want to give me a hand?" there was a hesitation before two men, Mr. Martin and his oldest son, Baxter, came forward to hold the box steady on the stool while Mr. Summers stirred up the papers inside it.

The original paraphernalia for the lottery had been lost long ago, and the black box now resting on the stool had been put into use even before Old Man Warner, the oldest man in town, was born. Mr. Summers spoke frequently to the villagers about making a new box, but no one liked to upset even as much tradition as was represented by the black box. There was a story that the present box had been made with some pieces of the box that had preceded it, the one that had been constructed when the first people settled down to make a village here. Every year, after the lottery, Mr. Summers began talking again about a new box, but every year the subject was allowed to fade off without anything's being done. The black box grew shabbier each year; by now it was no longer completely black but splintered badly along one side to show the original wood color, and in some places faded or stained.

Mr. Martin and his oldest son, Baxter, held the black box securely on the stool until Mr. Summers had stirred the papers thoroughly with his hand. Because so much of the ritual had been forgotten or discarded, Mr. Summers had been successful in having slips of paper substituted for the chips of wood that had been used for generations. Chips of wood, Mr. Summers had argued, had been all very well when the village was tiny, but now that the population was more than three hundred and likely to keep on growing, it was necessary to use something that would fit more easily into the black box. The night before the lottery, Mr. Summers and Mr. Graves made up the slips of paper and put them in the box, and it was then taken to the safe of Mr. Summers' coal company and locked up until Mr. Summers was ready to take it to the square next morning. The rest of the year, the box was put away, sometimes one place, sometimes another; it had spent one year in Mr. Graves's barn and another year underfoot in the post office, and sometimes it was set on a shelf in the Martin grocery and left there.

There was a great deal of fussing to be done before Mr. Summers declared the lottery open. There were the lists to make up—of heads of families, heads of households in each family, members of each household in each family. There was the proper swearing-in of Mr. Summers by the postmaster, as the official of the lottery; at one time, some people remembered, there had been a recital of some sort, performed by the official of the lottery, a perfunctory, tuneless chant that had been rattled off duly each year; some people believed that the official of the lottery used to stand just so when he said or sang it, others believed that he was supposed to walk among the people, but years and years ago this part of the ritual had been allowed to lapse. There had been, also, a ritual salute, which the official of the lottery had had to use in addressing each person who came up to draw from the box, but this also had changed with time, until now it was felt necessary only for the official to speak to each person approaching. Mr. Summers was very good at all this; in his clean white shirt and blue jeans, with one hand resting carelessly on the black box, he seemed very proper and important as he talked interminably to Mr. Graves and the Martins.

Just as Mr. Summers finally left off talking and turned to the assembled villagers, Mrs. Hutchinson came hurriedly along the path to the square, her sweater thrown over her shoulders, and slid into place in the back of the crowd. "Clean forgot what day it was," she said to Mrs. Delacroix, who stood next to her, and they both laughed softly. "Thought my old man was out back stacking wood," Mrs. Hutchinson went on, "and then I looked out the window and the kids were gone, and then I remembered it was the twenty-seventh and came a-running." She dried her hands on her apron, and Mrs. Delacroix said, "You're in time, though. They're still talking away up there."

Mrs. Hutchinson craned her neck to see through the crowd and found her husband and children standing near the front. She tapped Mrs. Delacroix on the arm as a farewell and began to make her way through the crowd. The people separated good-humoredly to let her through; two or three people said, in voices just loud enough to be heard across the crowd, "Here comes your Missus, Hutchinson," and "Bill, she made it after all." Mrs. Hutchinson reached her husband, and Mr. Summers, who had been waiting, said cheerfully, "Thought we were going to have to get

on without you, Tessie." Mrs. Hutchinson said, grinning, "Wouldn't have me leave m'dishes in the sink, now, would you, Joe?," and soft laughter ran through the crowd as the people stirred back into position after Mrs. Hutchinson's arrival.

"Well, now," Mr. Summers said soberly, "guess we better get started, get this over with, so's we can go back to work. Anybody ain't here?"

"Dunbar," several people said. "Dunbar, Dunbar."

Mr. Summers consulted his list. "Clyde Dunbar," he said. "That's right. He's broke his leg, hasn't he? Who's drawing for him?"

"Me, I guess," a woman said, and Mr. Summers turned to look at her. "Wife draws for her husband," Mr. Summers said. "Don't you have a grown boy to do it for you, Janey?" Although Mr. Summers and everyone else in the village knew the answer perfectly well, it was the business of the official of the lottery to ask such questions formally. Mr. Summers waited with an expression of polite interest while Mrs. Dunbar answered.

"Horace's not but sixteen yet," Mrs. Dunbar said regretfully. "Guess I gotta fill in for the old man this year."

"Right," Mr. Summers said. He made a note on the list he was holding. Then he asked, "Watson boy drawing this year?"

A tall boy in the crowd raised his hand. "Here," he said. "I'm drawing for m'mother and me." He blinked his eyes nervously and ducked his head as several voices in the crowd said things like "Good fellow, Jack," and "Glad to see your mother's got a man to do it."

"Well," Mr. Summers said, "guess that's everyone. Old Man Warner make it?"

"Here," a voice said, and Mr. Summers nodded.

A sudden hush fell on the crowd as Mr. Summers cleared his throat and looked at the list. "All ready?" he called. "Now, I'll read the names— heads of families first— and the men come up and take a paper out of the box. Keep the paper folded in your hand without looking at it until everyone has had a turn. Everything clear?"

The people had done it so many times that they only half listened to the directions; most of them were quiet, wetting their lips, not looking around. Then Mr. Summers raised one hand high and said, "Adams." A man disengaged himself from the crowd and came forward. "Hi, Steve," Mr. Summers said, and Mr. Adams said, "Hi, Joe." They grinned at one another humorlessly and nervously. Then Mr. Adams reached into the black box and took out a folded paper. He held it firmly by one corner as he turned and went hastily back to his place in the crowd, where he stood a little apart from his family, not looking down at his hand.

"Allen." Mr. Summers said. "Anderson … Bentham."

"Seems like there's no time at all between lotteries any more," Mrs. Delacroix said to Mrs. Graves in the back row. "Seems like we got through with the last one only last week."

"Time sure goes fast," Mrs. Graves said.

"Clark … Delacroix."

"There goes my old man," Mrs. Delacroix said. She held her breath while her husband went forward.

"Dunbar," Mr. Summers said, and Mrs. Dunbar went steadily to the box while one of the women said, "Go on, Janey," and another said, "There she goes."

"We're next," Mrs. Graves said. She watched while Mr. Graves came around from the side of the box, greeted Mrs. Summers gravely, and selected a slip of paper from the box. By now, all through the crowd there were men holding the small folded papers in their large hands, turning them over and over nervously. Mrs. Dunbar and her two sons stood together, Mrs. Dunbar holding the slip of paper.

"Harburt. … Hutchinson."

"Get up there, Bill," Mrs. Hutchinson said, and the people near her laughed.

"Jones."

"They do say," Mr. Adams said to Old Man Warner, who stood next to him, "that over in the north village they're talking of giving up the lottery."

Old Man Warner snorted. "Pack of crazy fools," he said. "Listening to the young folks, nothing's good enough for them. Next thing you know, they'll be wanting to go back to living in caves, nobody work any more, live that way for a while. Used to be a saying about 'Lottery in June, corn be heavy soon.' First thing you know, we'd all be eating stewed chickweed and acorns. There's always been a lottery," he added petulantly. "Bad enough to see young Joe Summers up there joking with everybody."

"Some places have already quit lotteries," Mrs. Adams said.

Nothing but trouble in that," Old Man Warner said stoutly. "Pack of young fools."

"Martin." And Bobby Martin watched his father go forward. "Overdyke. … Percy."

"I wish they'd hurry," Mrs. Dunbar said to her older son. "I wish they'd hurry."

"They're almost through," her son said.

"You get ready to run tell Dad," Mrs. Dunbar said.

Mr. Summers called his own name and then stepped forward precisely and selected a slip from the box. Then he called, "Warner."

"Seventy-seventh year I been in the lottery," Old Man Warner said as he went through the crowd. "Seventy-seventh time."

"Watson." The tall boy came awkwardly through the crowd. Someone said, "Don't be nervous, Jack." Mr. Summers said, "Take your time, son."

"Zanini."

After that, there was a long pause, a breathless pause, until Mr. Summers, holding his slip of paper in the air, said, "All right, fellows." For a minute, no one moved, and then all the slips of paper were opened. Suddenly, all the women began to speak at once, saying, "Who is it?,""Who's got it?,""Is it the Dunbars?,""Is it the Watsons?" Then the voices began to say, "It's Hutchinson. It's Bill,""Bill Hutchinson's got it."

"Go tell your father," Mrs. Dunbar said to her older son.

People began to look around to see the Hutchinsons. Bill Hutchinson was standing quiet, staring down at the paper in his hand. Suddenly, Tessie Hutchinson shouted to Mr. Summers, "You didn't give him time enough to take any paper he wanted. I saw you. It wasn't fair!"

"Be a good sport, Tessie," Mrs. Delacroix called, and Mrs. Graves said, "All of us took the same chance."

"Shut up, Tessie," Bill Hutchinson said.

"Well, everyone," Mr. Summers said, "that was done pretty fast, and now we've got to be hurrying a little more to get it done in time." He consulted his next list. "Bill," he said, "you draw for the Hutchinson family. You got any other households in the Hutchinsons?"

"There's Don and Eva," Mrs. Hutchinson yelled. "Make them take their chance!"

"Daughters draw with their husbands' families, Tessie," Mr. Summers said gently. "You know that as well as anyone else."

"I guess not, Joe," Bill Hutchinson said regretfully. "My daughter draws with her husband's family, that's only fair. And I've got no other family except the kids."

"Then, as far as drawing for families is concerned, it's you," Mr. Summers said in explanation, "and as far as drawing for households is concerned, that's you, too. Right?"

"Right," Bill Hutchinson said.

"How many kids, Bill?" Mr. Summers asked formally.

"Three," Bill Hutchinson said. "There's Bill, Jr., and Nancy, and little Dave. And Tessie and me."

"All right, then," Mr. Summers said. "Harry, you got their tickets back?"

Mr. Graves nodded and held up the slips of paper. "Put them in the box, then," Mr. Summers directed. "Take Bill's and put it in."

"I think we ought to start over," Mrs. Hutchinson said, as quietly as she could. "I tell you it wasn't fair. You didn't give him time enough to choose. Everybody saw that."

Mr. Graves had selected the five slips and put them in the box, and he dropped all the papers but those onto the ground, where the breeze caught them and lifted them off.

"Listen, everybody," Mrs. Hutchinson was saying to the people around her.

"Ready, Bill?" Mr. Summers asked, and Bill Hutchinson, with one quick glance around at his wife and children, nodded.

"Remember," Mr. Summers said, "take the slips and keep them folded until each person has taken one. Harry, you help little Dave." Mr. Graves took the hand of the little boy, who came willingly with him up to the box. "Take a paper out of the box, Davy," Mr. Summers said. Davy put his hand into the box and laughed. "Take just one paper," Mr. Summers said. "Harry, you hold it for him." Mr. Graves took the child's hand and removed the folded paper from the tight fist and held it while little Dave stood next to him and looked up at him wonderingly.

"Nancy next," Mr. Summers said. Nancy was twelve, and her school friends breathed heavily as she went forward, switching her skirt, and took a slip daintily from the box. "Bill, Jr.," Mr. Summers said, and Billy, his face red and his feet over-large, nearly knocked the box over as he got a paper out. "Tessie," Mr. Summers said. She hesitated for a minute, looking around defiantly, and then set her lips and went up to the box. She snatched a paper out and held it behind her.

"Bill," Mr. Summers said, and Bill Hutchinson reached into the box and felt around, bringing his hand out at last with the slip of paper in it.

The crowd was quiet. A girl whispered, "I hope it's not Nancy," and the sound of the whisper reached the edges of the crowd.

"It's not the way it used to be," Old Man Warner said clearly. "People ain't the way they used to be."

"All right," Mr. Summers said. "Open the papers. Harry, you open little Dave's."

Mr. Graves opened the slip of paper and there was a general sigh through the crowd as he held it up and everyone could see that it was blank. Nancy and Bill, Jr., opened theirs at the same time, and both beamed and laughed, turning around to the crowd and holding their slips of paper above their heads.

"Tessie," Mr. Summers said. There was a pause, and then Mr. Summers looked at Bill Hutchinson, and Bill unfolded his paper and showed it. It was blank.

"It's Tessie," Mr. Summers said, and his voice was hushed. "Show us her paper, Bill."

Bill Hutchinson went over to his wife and forced the slip of paper out of her hand. It had a black spot on it, the black spot Mr. Summers had made the night before with the heavy pencil in the coal-company office. Bill Hutchinson held it up, and there was a stir in the crowd.

"All right, folks," Mr. Summers said. "Let's finish quickly." Although the villagers had forgotten the ritual and lost the original black box, they still remembered to use stones. The pile of stones the boys had made earlier was ready; there were stones on the ground with the blowing scraps of paper that had come out of the box. Mrs. Delacroix selected a stone so large she had to pick it up with both hands and turned to Mrs. Dunbar. "Come on," she said. "Hurry up."

Mrs. Dunbar had small stones in both hands, and she said, gasping for breath, "I can't run at all. You'll have to go ahead and I'll catch up with you."

The children had stones already, and someone gave little Davy Hutchinson a few pebbles.

Tessie Hutchinson was in the center of a cleared space by now, and she held her hands out desperately as the villagers moved in on her. "It isn't fair," she said. A stone hit her on the side of the head.

Old Man Warner was saying, "Come on, come on, everyone." Steve Adams was in the front of the crowd of villagers, with Mrs. Graves beside him.

"It isn't fair, it isn't right," Mrs. Hutchinson screamed, and then they were upon her.

Name: _____ Date: _____

Vocabulary Web

Directions: Complete the Vocabulary Web for *paraphernalia*.

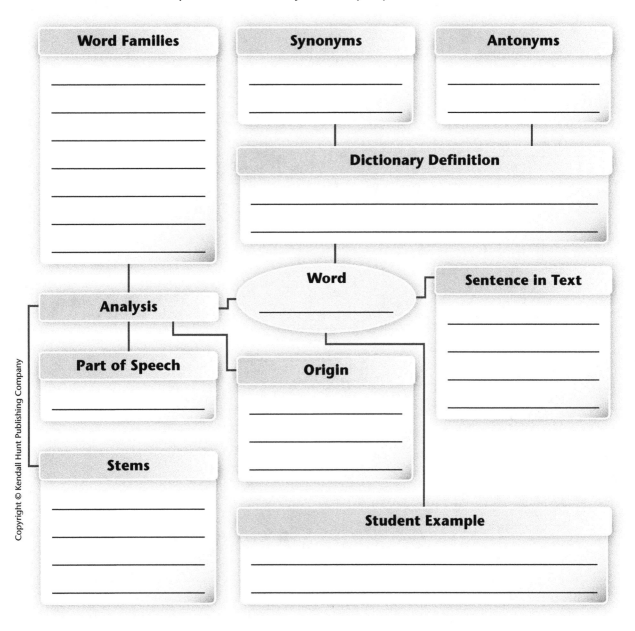

Name: _____ Date: _____

Activity
1B

Vocabulary Web

Directions: Complete the Vocabulary Web for one of the following words from "The Lottery": *perfunctory, reprimand,* or *interminably.*

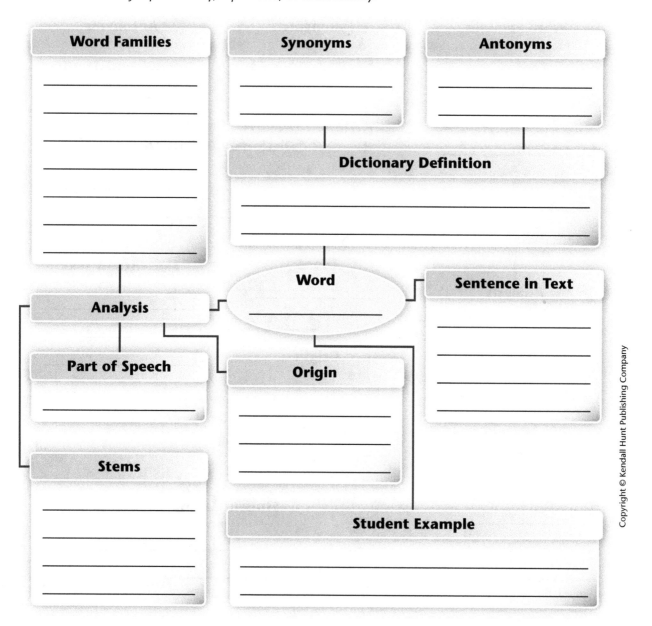

Word Families

Synonyms

Antonyms

Dictionary Definition

Word

Sentence in Text

Analysis

Part of Speech

Origin

Stems

Student Example

Name: _____ Date: _____

Activity

Independent Reading Assignment

Directions: During the unit, you will read several books independently and complete some activities to bring to a class discussion of the books. The books to be read independently are:

Anne Frank: The Diary of a Young Girl by Anne Frank
Maus II by Art Spiegelman
The Member of the Wedding by Carson McCullers
Hiroshima by John Hersey

Please complete the following activities for each of the books you read:

1. Complete a **Literature Web** for a section of the book (Literature Webs will be introduced in Lesson 5).

2. Keep a list of vocabulary words in the book that are new words for you. Make **Vocabulary Webs** for at least two of the words.

3. After approximately every 30 pages you read, stop and write a journal entry of your own. Share your reactions to what you are reading and your thoughts about the issues raised in the book.

4. When you have completed the book, write a synopsis of no more than 100 words that would tell a reader interested in the book the main points they might wish to consider when deciding whether to read it.

Optional Extension

For each book, create some kind of advertisement to persuade someone to read it. You might create a new book jacket, design a newspaper advertisement, or write a review of the book.

Assignment Schedule

Book #	Title	Lesson Due	Date Due
1	*Anne Frank: The Diary of a Young Girl* by Anne Frank	Lesson 7	
2	*Maus II* by Art Spiegelman	Lesson 13	
3	*The Member of the Wedding* by Carson McCullers	Lesson 17	
4	*Hiroshima* by John Hersey	Lesson 19	

Name: _____ Date: _____

 **Activity**
1D

Directions: Complete a Literature Web about a section from *Anne Frank: The Diary of a Young Girl.*

Key Words
_____
_____
_____
_____
_____

Feelings
_____
_____
_____
_____
_____

Ideas
_____
_____
_____
_____
_____
_____

Title
_____
_____
_____

Images/Symbols
_____
_____
_____
_____
_____
_____

Structure
_____
_____
_____
_____

Name: _____ Date: _____

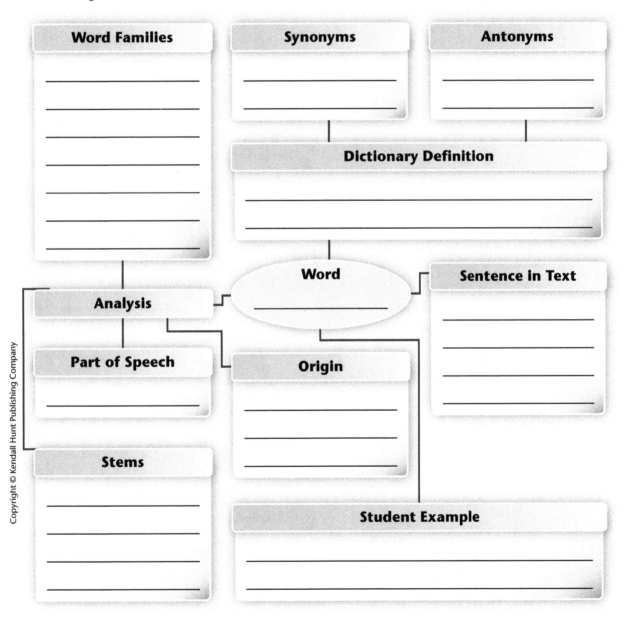
Vocabulary Web

Directions: Complete the Vocabulary Web for a word from *Anne Frank: The Diary of a Young Girl.*

Word Families	**Synonyms**	**Antonyms**

Dictionary Definition

Word

Analysis

Sentence in Text

Part of Speech

Origin

Stems

Student Example

Activity
1F

Directions: Complete the Vocabulary Web for a word from *Anne Frank: The Diary of a Young Girl.*

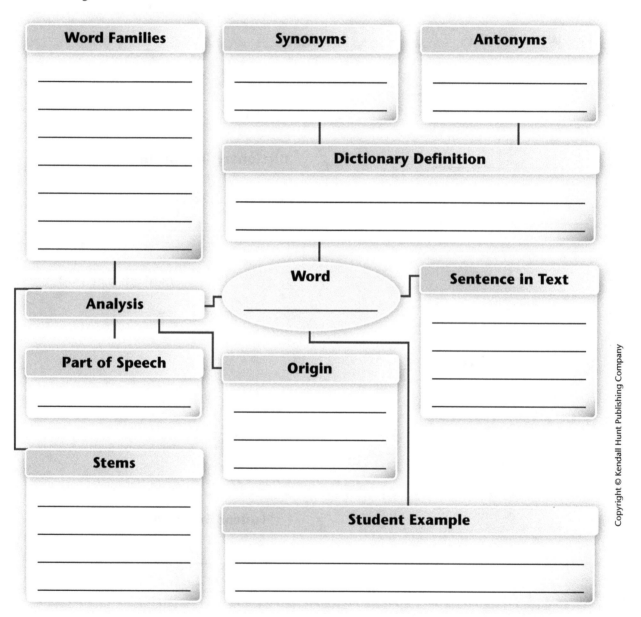

Word Families

Synonyms

Antonyms

Dictionary Definition

Word

Sentence in Text

Analysis

Part of Speech

Origin

Stems

Student Example

Name: _____ Date: _____

Change Model

Directions: Develop a list of three examples for each of the following statements (generalizations) about change.

Change

> **Change is linked to time.**
>
> _____
> _____
> _____

> **Change is everywhere.**
>
> _____
> _____
> _____

> **Change may be positive or negative.**
>
> _____
> _____
> _____

> **Change may be perceived as orderly or random.**
>
> _____
> _____
> _____

> **Change may happen naturally or may be caused by people.**
>
> _____
> _____
> _____

 **Activity**

Essay: Defend a Generalization

Directions: Write a five-paragraph essay arguing that one of the generalizations about change is true. In your essay, you should give at least three reasons to support your main idea and explain your reasons carefully. Use specific examples to elaborate on your reasons. Include a strong conclusion in your essay.

Name: _____ Date: _____

Nuclear Energy:
A Positive or Negative Change?

Directions: Work with your group to list examples of how nuclear energy has been used or specific historical events relating to its use. Discuss with your group in which column each example should be placed.

Positive	Negative	Both

Name: _____ Date: _____

1940s Information Web

Directions: Brainstorm what you already know about the 1940s. Use this web as a starting point to expand the categories and the specific examples.

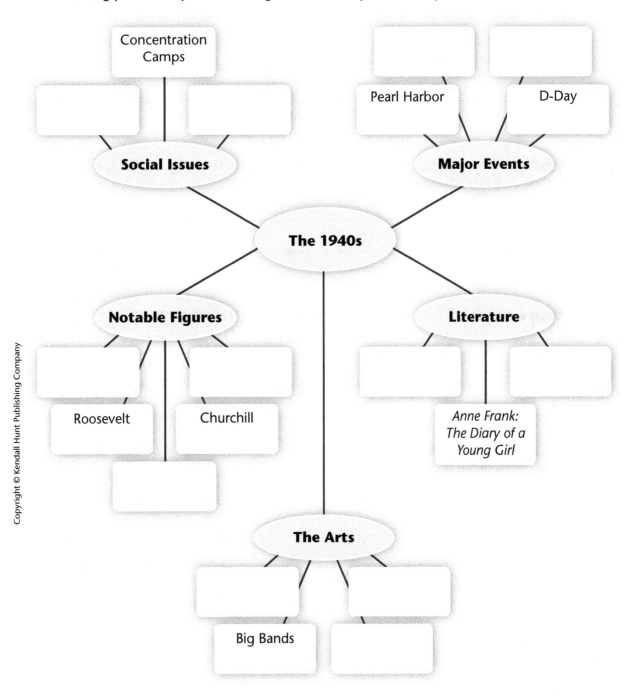

Name: _____ Date: _____

 **Activity**

Directions: Respond to these questions based on the speech(es) by Franklin D. Roosevelt.

1. What was the speaker's general purpose (to inform, to persuade, to entertain, to inspire)?

_____

_____

_____

2. What was the speaker's specific thesis? What were the individual goals the speaker hoped to achieve through the presentation?

_____

_____

_____

3. What were some of the main points or ideas mentioned by the speaker?

_____

_____

_____

4. What were some key words or sentences that you found particularly memorable or effective from the speech?

_____

_____

_____

Name: _____ Date: _____

Activity

Speech Analysis Form

Directions: Respond to these questions based on the speech(es) by Winston Churchill.

1. What was the speaker's general purpose (to inform, to persuade, to entertain, to inspire)?

   _____

   _____

   _____

2. What was the speaker's specific thesis? What were the individual goals the speaker hoped to achieve through the presentation?

   _____

   _____

   _____

3. What were some of the main points or ideas mentioned by the speaker?

   _____

   _____

   _____

4. What were some key words or sentences that you found particularly memorable or effective from the speech?

   _____

   _____

   _____

Name: _____ Date: _____

Interview Assignment

Directions: Contact a person in your family or community who lived during the 1940s and was old enough at that time to have a good memory about what society was like and the changes which took place as a result of the major events facing the world. You may have several family members or friends who might be willing to be interviewed, or you may wish to visit a local retirement home and ask if there is anyone who would be willing to discuss the time period with you. Explain to the person that you are studying the 1940s and the changes which took place during that time, and that you would like to interview him or her to find out about his or her perspective on that period of history.

Use the **Interview Preparation Guidelines** (Activity 4B) to help you in planning and conducting your interview. After you interview the person, write 2 to 3 pages to describe what you learned. Prepare one of the stories your interviewee tells you to share orally with the class in Lesson 18.

Name: _____ Date: _____

 **Activity**

Directions: Follow these guidelines to help you prepare for your interview.

Selecting an Interviewee

You might choose to interview a grandparent or other family member who remembers the 1940s, or a friend from your community or school. You might also choose to visit a local retirement home and ask if someone would be willing to be interviewed.

Listening

What are some ways to be an active listener? What are some phrases and questions you can use to encourage people to give you more information about something? (e.g., "That sounds really interesting." "Can you give me an example?" "Can you tell me more?") What are some actions involved with being a courteous listener? (e.g., Do not rush the interviewee; do not disagree with the person you are interviewing; do not interrupt.) Remember that your interviewee may be an elderly person, and it is always important to show respect for whomever you are interviewing. You will also be asking about a time in which many sad things happened, and your interviewee may have some painful memories. Be sensitive to your interviewee's feelings.

Questions

The questions you ask will determine what kind and the amount of information you receive. Consider what you know about the person you are interviewing and what more you want to know about that person and his or her experiences in the 1940s, and think of some questions. Remember the **purpose** of your interview and keep your questions focused around that. Open-ended questions, rather than yes/no questions or questions needing just a one-word answer, will usually give you more interesting answers.

Even though you should write questions in advance, be prepared to make up new ones to follow up on what the person tells you once he or she starts talking with you. Later in the interview, feel free to return to earlier questions if they need to be clarified.

Be sure to give your interviewee a chance to tell you something that would be of interest but that you didn't think of when you were writing your questions. You may want to include a question such as the following: "Is there anything else that you would like to tell me about or that might be of interest to my class and people my age?"

The following are some questions you might want to think about including in your interview. Add your own questions to those given.

- *What was your life like in the 1940s? What kind of job/school were you working at or attending?*

- *What effects did the war have on your community?*

- *Tell me about the music and the movies of the 1940s. How did you like to spend your free time?*

- *What aspects of your life changed as a result of the events of the 1940s? How did your community change?*

- *Tell me your favorite story about something that happened to you in the 1940s.*

Name: _____ Date: _____

 **Activity**

Directions: Summarize the picture book you read by responding to the following prompts.

Book Title: _____ **Author:** _____

Summarizing Practice

1. Make a works cited entry for the book. Use MLA style format.

_____

_____

_____

2. Write down the most important ideas, themes, symbols, etc., that you found in this book.

_____

_____

_____

_____

_____

3. Select one or more statements that seem important or significant. Copy these word for word and put quotation marks around them. Provide the page number.

_____

_____

_____

_____

_____

_____

4. On another sheet of paper, create a Concept Web about the picture book.

5. Using your Concept Web, write a one-paragraph summary of the book.

_____

_____

_____

_____

_____

_____

Name: _____ Date: _____

 **Activity**

Directions: Summarize the picture book you read by responding to the following prompts.

Book Title: _____ **Author:** _____

Summarizing Practice

1. Make a works cited entry for the book. Use MLA style format.

_____

_____

_____

2. Write down the most important ideas, themes, symbols, etc., that you found in this book.

_____

_____

_____

_____

_____

_____

3. Select one or more statements that seem important or significant. Copy these word for word and put quotation marks around them. Provide the page number.

_____

_____

_____

_____

_____

4. On another sheet of paper, create a Concept Web about the picture book.

5. Using your Concept Web, write a one-paragraph summary of the book.

_____

_____

_____

_____

_____

_____

Name: _____ Date: _____

 **Activity**

Interview Analysis Form

Directions: Use this page to take notes about an interview. Pay close attention to the interviewer's behavior.

Purpose

What was the purpose of the interview?

_____

_____

_____

_____

_____

_____

Questions

What were some of the most effective questions the interviewer asked? Why were they effective?

_____

_____

_____

_____

_____

_____

Follow-up

How did the interviewer follow up on the guest's responses—by asking additional questions, by commenting, etc.? What techniques did the interviewer use to encourage the guest to elaborate?

_____

_____

_____

_____

_____

_____

Facial Expressions/Body Language

Describe the interviewer's facial expressions and/or body language. How might these have affected the person being interviewed?

_____

_____

_____

_____

_____

_____

Other

Describe any other details you noticed or impressions you had about the interviewer.

_____

_____

_____

_____

_____

_____

Statistics

Carl Sandburg

Napoleon shifted,
Restless in the old sarcophagus
And murmured to a watchguard:
"Who goes there?"
"Twenty-one million men,
Soldiers, armies, guns,
Twenty-one million
Afoot, horseback,
In the air,
Under the sea."
And Napoleon turned to his sleep:
"It is not my world answering;
It is some dreamer who knows not
The world I marched in
From Calais to Moscow."
And he slept on
In the old sarcophagus
While the aeroplanes
Droned their motors
Between Napoleon's mausoleum
And the cool night stars.

"Statistics" from *Chicago Poems* by Carl Sandburg, copyright 1916 by Holt, Rinehart and Winston, Inc. and renewed 1944 by Carl Sandburg, reprinted by permission of Harcourt Brace & Company.

Grass

Carl Sandburg

Pile the bodies high at Austerlitz and Waterloo.
Shovel them under and let me work—
I am the grass; I cover all.

And pile them high at Gettysburg
And pile them high at Ypres and Verdun.
Shovel them under and let me work.
Two years, ten years, and passengers ask the
conductor:
  What place is this?
  Where are we now?

I am the grass,
Let me work.

"Grass" from *Cornhuskers* by Carl Sandburg, copyright 1918 by Holt, Rinehart and Winston, Inc. and renewed 1946 by Carl Sandburg, reprinted by permission of Harcourt Brace & Company.

Name: _____   Date: _____

Literature Web

Directions: Complete a Literature Web about "Statistics."

Key Words	Feelings
_____	_____
_____	_____
_____	_____
_____	_____
_____	_____

Ideas
_____
_____
_____
_____
_____
_____
_____

Title
_____
_____
_____
_____

Images/Symbols
_____
_____
_____
_____
_____
_____
_____

Structure
_____
_____
_____
_____

Name: _____ Date: _____

 **Activity**
5B

Directions: Complete a Literature Web about "Grass."

Key Words	**Feelings**
_____	_____
_____	_____
_____	_____
_____	_____
_____	_____
_____	_____

Ideas

_____
_____
_____
_____
_____
_____

Title

_____
_____
_____
_____

Images/Symbols

_____
_____
_____
_____
_____
_____
_____
_____

Structure

_____
_____
_____
_____

Name: _____ Date: _____

Activity

Need to Know Board

Directions: Use the Need to Know Board to determine what you know about the battles named in the poem "Grass," what you would like to know, and where you can find the information.

What Do We Know?	What Do We Need to Know?	How Can We Find Out?

Name: _____ Date: _____

Why You Should Become a Vegetarian

Directions: Review this persuasive writing sample and analyze its components for the Hamburger Model structure. Compare the sample paragraph with the structure used in the model.

I believe that more people should become vegetarians for many reasons. Most importantly, eating meat hurts defenseless animals. They are often raised and transported in uncomfortable conditions, and then they are killed. There are also health reasons not to eat meat. Studies show that vegetarians are less likely to have heart disease and cancer. A third reason is that it takes more natural resources to raise meat than other foods such as fruits and vegetables. Not only do you have to raise the cattle, you have to raise the food to feed the cattle. For these reasons I hope that people who eat meat will rethink their eating habits and consider becoming vegetarian.

Name: _____ Date: _____

 Activity

Directions: Identify the elements of the paragraph "Why You Should Become a Vegetarian" that belong in each part of the Hamburger Model. Write each element of the paragraph in the appropriate part of the model.

**Introduction
(State your opinion.)**

_____
_____

Elaboration	**Elaboration**	**Elaboration**
_____	_____	_____
_____	_____	_____
_____	_____	_____

Reason	**Reason**	**Reason**
_____	_____	_____
_____	_____	_____
_____	_____	_____

Elaboration	**Elaboration**	**Elaboration**
_____	_____	_____
_____	_____	_____
_____	_____	_____

Conclusion

_____
_____

Name: _____ Date: _____

Hamburger Model
for Persuasive Writing

Activity

Directions: Use the Hamburger Model to organize ideas for your essay.

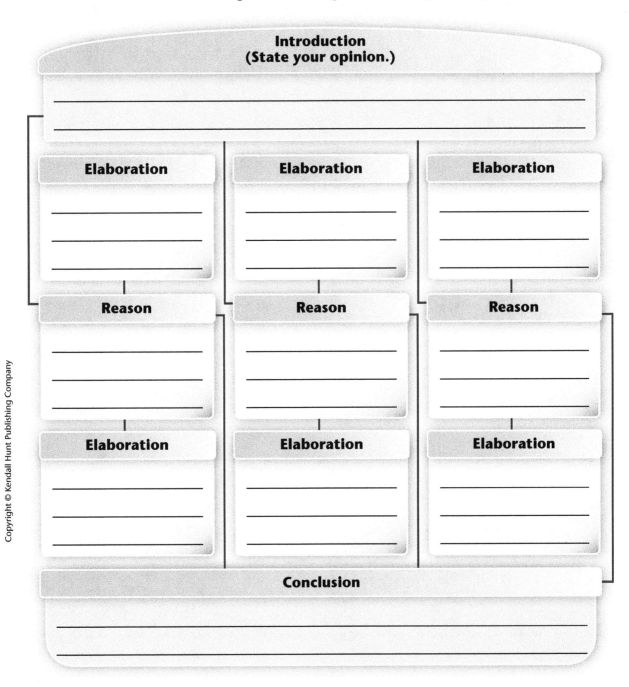

 **Activity**
6D

Directions: Review the Dagwood Model for Persuasive Writing. The structure is like that of the Hamburger Model except that it addresses more details. In particular, it addresses other points of view.

Claim/Opinion/Introduction

| Details | Background | Details |

Reason

Elaboration

Other Points of View

Elaboration

Reason

Elaboration

Other Points of View

Elaboration

Reason

Elaboration

Other Points of View

Elaboration

Conclusion

Name: _____ Date: _____

Activity

Sample Persuasive Essay

Directions: Read the following paragraph. Highlight and label your opinion (the top bun), the reasons (meat) and supporting evidence (fixings), and the conclusion (bottom bun).

Capital Punishment

In recent years capital punishment has been invoked in many states. I believe that it should be abolished because it is immoral, ineffective as a deterrent to crime, and subject to risky decision-making.

First, two wrongs don't make a right. To kill someone convicted of murder contradicts the reasoning behind the law that taking another's life is wrong. The Bible tells us that killing is wrong in the Commandment "Thou shalt not kill." In capital punishment, the state is committing the same violent act that it is condemning.

Second, the death penalty is not as effective a deterrent to the crime as some people want it to be. Many studies show that murderers do not think about the consequences of their actions when they commit the crime; they show that murder is usually a result of complex sociological and psychological problems that make the murderer act out of need for immediate gratification.

The third and most serious objection is that death is final and cannot be altered. Errors in deciding guilt or innocence will always be present in our system of trial by jury. There is too great a risk that innocent people will be put to death. If even one person is put to death by mistake, it would be too many.

Putting murderers in prison for life seems the best alternative for those who commit murder. It keeps dangerous people away from society while it avoids the problems of making an irrevocable mistake and of having to decide "life and death." Too much is at stake here to continue the practice of capital punishment.

Name: _____ Date: _____

 **Activity**

Directions: The writing process is not merely putting words down on paper. Some writers need a structure that allows them to organize their prewriting in stages to prepare for their first draft. If you struggle to know where to begin, this planner may assist you.

Content: What will be the subject of your paper? _____

Ideas: Try stating your position. Remember, this should not just be a fact, but a debatable point that is clear and concise. Write your first position draft sentence now.

_____

_____

Reasons: What are the three best reasons to support your position? List them.

1. _____

2. _____

3. _____

Support: For each of your reasons, what are specific pieces of evidence, examples, and statistics that can encourage the reader to believe as you do? Avoid broad generalizations and personal opinions to persuade the reader. Remember, support may include facts, statistics, quotes, or examples. Facts are a powerful way to convince readers to consider your position as the one they should hold. Facts may be gathered from reading sources, observation, or personal experience. Statistics often strengthen your position. Evaluate your sources carefully. Be sure to cite your sources. Quotes, especially direct quotes from reliable sources, can help support your position exceptionally well. Again, be sure to cite your sources. Examples help make your ideas concrete for the reader.

Reason one support:

_____

_____

Reason two support:

_____

_____

Reason three support:

_____

_____

Now you are ready to put these ideas together into your essay. Remember to try to grab your reader's attention. Consider your audience.

Name: _____ Date: _____

 **Activity**
6G

Directions: Review the Writing Process. Begin the prewriting phase for an essay arguing for or against a cigarette ban in public places.

The Writing Process describes the stages that writers use to develop a written composition. The stages are not separate parts that writers go through from one to five; rather, writers move back and forth among the stages and use them to construct, clarify, and polish their writing. The Writing Process Model is used throughout the unit to encourage you to improve your own writing.

1. *Prewriting:* List your ideas and begin to organize them. You may want to use a graphic organizer such as a web or a Venn diagram. Graphic organizers help you to "see" what you will write about in your essay. As you write, you can add to your diagram or change it.

2. *Drafting:* Write a rough draft, getting your ideas onto paper without worrying about mechanics such as spelling, grammar, or punctuation. Some writers call this stage "composing." Sometimes the first draft is a "messing around" stage in which your drafting or composing helps you to "hear" what you want to say.

3. *Revising:* Conferencing is an essential step in the revising stage. Ask people (friends, family, teachers) to read and listen to your work and to tell you what they like, what they don't understand, and what they'd like to know more about. This is the place to make major changes in your "composition" or draft. Sometimes you may want to go back to the prewriting stage and redo your organizer so that your paper has a new structure.

4. *Editing:* After you have revised your paper, look for the small changes that will make a big difference. Check your choice of words and identify mechanical errors. After you make the changes and corrections, proofread your work one final time. You may want to ask a friend or an adult for help.

5. *Sharing or Publishing:* There are numerous ways to share and to publish your work. You can bind it into a book, post it on a blog, or submit it to a writing contest.

Name: _____ Date: _____

Hamburger Model
for Persuasive Writing

Activity

Directions: Use the Hamburger Model for Persuasive Writing to organize ideas for an essay arguing for or against a cigarette ban in public places.

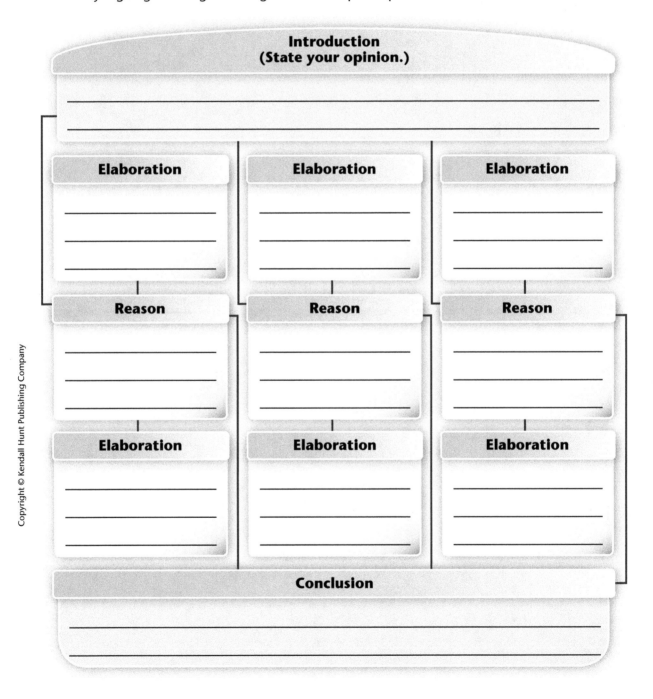

Introduction
(State your opinion.)

_____
_____

| **Elaboration** | **Elaboration** | **Elaboration** |

| **Reason** | **Reason** | **Reason** |

| **Elaboration** | **Elaboration** | **Elaboration** |

Conclusion

_____
_____

Name: _____ Date: _____

Self-Review of Writing

Assignment: _____

Directions: Evaluate your own writing. For each sentence below, circle the choice that best describes your writing. Then complete the two sentences.

1. My main idea is clear.

   Needs improvement   Satisfactory   Excellent

2. My details support the main idea.

   Needs improvement   Satisfactory   Excellent

3. My ideas flow smoothly and in an orderly way.

   Needs improvement   Satisfactory   Excellent

4. The structure clearly follows the Hamburger Model (introduction, body, conclusion).

   Needs improvement   Satisfactory   Excellent

5. My vocabulary is rich and varied.

   Needs improvement   Satisfactory   Excellent

My writing is strong in these ways:

_____

_____

_____

My writing could be improved in these ways:

_____

_____

_____

Name: _____ Date: _____

 **Activity**
78

Peer Review of Writing

Writer: _____ **Assignment:** _____

Directions: Evaluate your partner's writing. For each sentence, circle the choice that best describes the writing. Then complete the two sentences.

1. The main idea is clear.

   Needs improvement   Satisfactory   Excellent

2. The details support the main idea.

   Needs improvement   Satisfactory   Excellent

3. The ideas flow smoothly and in an orderly way.

   Needs improvement   Satisfactory   Excellent

4. The structure clearly follows the Hamburger Model (introduction, body, conclusion).

   Needs improvement   Satisfactory   Excellent

5. The vocabulary is rich and varied.

   Needs improvement   Satisfactory   Excellent

The writing is strong in these ways:

_____

_____

_____

The writing could be improved in these ways:

_____

_____

_____

Copyright © Kendall Hunt Publishing Company

Name: _____ Date: _____

 **Activity**

Literature Web

Directions: Complete a Literature Web about a section from *Maus II.*

Key Words
_____
_____
_____
_____
_____

Feelings
_____
_____
_____
_____
_____

Ideas
_____
_____
_____
_____
_____
_____

Title
_____
_____
_____
_____

Images/Symbols
_____
_____
_____
_____
_____
_____
_____

Structure
_____
_____
_____
_____

Name: _____ Date: _____

 **Activity**
7D

Directions: Complete the Vocabulary Web for a word from *Maus II*.

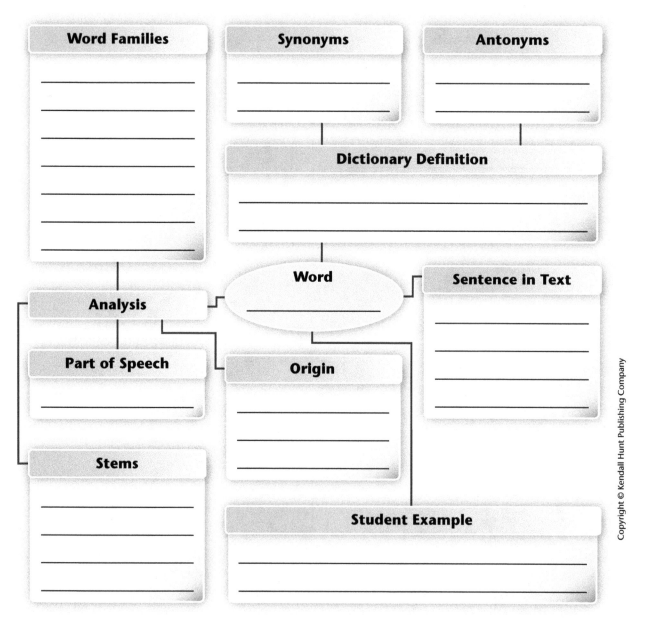

Word Families

Synonyms

Antonyms

Dictionary Definition

Analysis

Word

Sentence in Text

Part of Speech

Origin

Stems

Student Example

Name: _____ Date: _____

Activity

Vocabulary Web

Directions: Complete the Vocabulary Web for a word from *Maus II*.

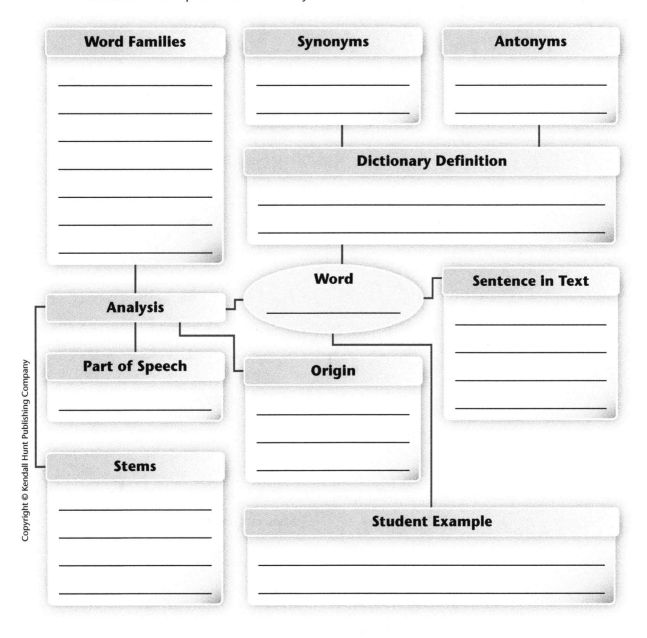

Word Families	Synonyms	Antonyms

Dictionary Definition

Word

Analysis

Sentence in Text

Part of Speech

Origin

Stems

Student Example

 **Activity**
7F

Directions: Complete the Vocabulary Web for the word *holocaust.*

Word Families
_____
_____
_____
_____
_____
_____

Synonyms
_____
_____

Antonyms
_____
_____

Dictionary Definition
_____
_____

Word
_____

Analysis

Part of Speech
_____

Origin
_____
_____

Sentence in Text
_____
_____
_____

Stems
_____
_____
_____

Student Example
_____
_____

Name: _____ Date: _____

Elements of Reasoning

Directions: Review the Elements of Reasoning. (See detailed definitions in the section of this book titled "Models.") These elements can help you to think and argue better.

1. *Purpose or Goal:* When we speak or write, it should be for a purpose. That purpose should be clear, achievable, and realistic. For example, it might be to inform, to persuade, to entertain, or to inspire.

2. *Issue or Problem:* When we reason, there must be some issue or question that needs to be resolved. As part of the reasoning process, we should be able to formulate the question to be answered or the issue to be addressed.

3. *Point of View:* We must reason from some point of view or frame of reference. If the point of view is too narrow, it may be restricted or unfair. The consideration of other points of view may sharpen or broaden our thinking.

4. *Experiences, Data, or Evidence:* We must have data, evidence, or experiences on which to base our reasoning. Evidence is important in order to distinguish opinions from reasons or to create a reasoned judgment. It needs to be accurate, fair, and clear to ensure good reasoning.

5. *Concepts or Ideas:* All reasoning uses some ideas, terms, principles, and rules and not others. When we read and listen, we can ask ourselves, "What are the key ideas presented?" When we write and speak, we can examine and organize our thoughts around the substance of concepts and ideas.

6. *Assumptions:* We take some things for granted when we reason. We need to be aware of the assumptions we have made and the assumptions of others. Incorrect assumptions can be the source of faulty reasoning.

7. *Inferences or Interpretations:* Reasoning proceeds by steps called inferences. An inference is a small step of the mind, in which a person concludes that something is so because of something else being so or seeming to be so. We need to distinguish between the raw data of our experiences and our interpretations of those experiences (inferences). The inferences we make are heavily influenced by our point of view and our assumptions.

8. *Implications and Consequences:* When we reason in a certain direction, we need to consider the consequences of that direction. When we argue and support a certain point of view, solid reasoning requires that we consider what the implications are of following that path. The ability to reason well is measured in part by an ability to understand and identify the implications and consequences of the reasoning.

Name: _____ Date: _____

 **Activity**

Directions: Take notes responding to each question as your teacher thinks aloud about a problem.

1. **Purpose or Goal:** What is the **purpose** of reasoning about this situation?

   _____

   _____

   _____

2. **Issue or Problem:** What is the **issue** or **problem** with which I am dealing?

   _____

   _____

   _____

3. **Point of View:** What would each of the people (or animals) involved think about the problem? What are the **points of view** of the various stakeholders?

   _____

   _____

   _____

4. **Experiences, Data, or Evidence:** What **facts** and **evidence** will help me solve the problem?

   _____

   _____

   _____

5. **Concepts or Ideas:** What **concepts** or big **ideas** are involved in this problem?

_____

_____

_____

6. **Assumptions:** What **assumptions** might I or other stakeholders make about the situation?

_____

_____

_____

7. **Inferences:** What are some **inferences** or **small conclusions** I can make based on the facts I have?

_____

_____

_____

8. **Implications and Consequences:** What are the **implications** of following a certain line of reasoning?

_____

_____

_____

Name: _____ Date: _____

 **Activity**
8C

Standards of Reasoning

Directions: Use the questions to evaluate the argument in the sample persuasive essay on capital punishment (Activity 6E). Apply these standards to the essay to determine whether you think the author developed a well-reasoned argument. Answer the questions in the spaces provided.

1. **Clarity:** Are the reasons clear? Are they elaborated well? Is the meaning understandable by anyone who reads this? Are illustrations or examples included?

   _____

   _____

   _____

   _____

2. **Accuracy:** Is the evidence correct or right?

   _____

   _____

   _____

   _____

3. **Precision:** Are specific reasons or examples included rather than vague generalizations?

   _____

   _____

   _____

   _____

Adapted from Paul, R. (1992). *Critical thinking: What every person needs to know to survive in a rapidly changing world.* Sonoma, CA: Foundation for Critical Thinking.

Copyright © Kendall Hunt Publishing Company

70   *The 1940s: A Decade of Change · Lesson 8 · Reasoning*

4. **Relevance:** How is what the author says connected to the question? Is it important for the issue?

_____

_____

_____

_____

5. **Depth:** How does the author address the complexities in the question? Are the arguments and reasons strong and important, or do they seem to be superficial?

_____

_____

_____

_____

6. **Breadth:** Has the author looked at enough different points of view? Is there another way to look at this question?

_____

_____

_____

_____

7. **Logic:** Does this make sense? Is the thinking logical? Does the argument follow an understandable path or is it just a disconnected group of statements?

_____

_____

_____

_____

Name: _____ Date: _____

 Activity

Directions: Use the Hamburger Model to organize ideas for your essay responding to this prompt: *Should middle school students wear uniforms to school?*

**Introduction
(State your opinion.)**

_____

_____

Elaboration	**Elaboration**	**Elaboration**
_____	_____	_____
_____	_____	_____
_____	_____	_____

Reason	**Reason**	**Reason**
_____	_____	_____
_____	_____	_____
_____	_____	_____

Elaboration	**Elaboration**	**Elaboration**
_____	_____	_____
_____	_____	_____
_____	_____	_____

Conclusion

_____

_____

Name: _____ Date: _____

Activity

Standards of Reasoning

Directions: Use the questions to evaluate the argument in the newspaper editorial you chose. Answer the questions in the spaces provided.

1. **Clarity:** Are the reasons clear? Are they elaborated well? Is the meaning understandable by anyone who reads this? Are illustrations or examples included?

_____

_____

_____

_____

2. **Accuracy:** Is the evidence correct or right?

_____

_____

_____

_____

3. **Precision:** Are specific reasons or examples included rather than vague generalizations?

_____

_____

_____

_____

Adapted from Paul, R. (1992). *Critical thinking: What every person needs to know to survive in a rapidly changing world.* Sonoma, CA: Foundation for Critical Thinking.

4. Relevance: How is what the author says connected to the question? Is it important for the issue?

_____

_____

_____

_____

5. Depth: How does the author address the complexities in the question? Are the arguments and reasons strong and important, or do they seem to be superficial?

_____

_____

_____

_____

6. Breadth: Has the author looked at enough different points of view? Is there another way to look at this question?

_____

_____

_____

_____

7. Logic: Does this make sense? Is the thinking logical? Does the argument follow an understandable path or is it just a disconnected group of statements?

_____

_____

_____

_____

Name: _____ Date: _____

Activity
9A

Literature Web

Directions: Complete a Literature Web about "Serving Mein Führer" from the *Voices of the Holocaust* anthology.

Key Words	Feelings
_____	_____
_____	_____
_____	_____
_____	_____
_____	_____

Ideas	Title	Images/Symbols
_____	_____	_____
_____	_____	_____
_____	_____	_____
_____	_____	_____
_____		_____

Structure

_____

_____

_____

Name: _____ Date: _____

 Activity

Directions: Complete a Literature Web about "A Survivor Remembers" from the *Voices of the Holocaust* anthology.

Key Words
_____
_____
_____
_____
_____

Feelings
_____
_____
_____
_____
_____

Ideas
_____
_____
_____
_____
_____

Title
_____
_____
_____
_____

Images/Symbols
_____
_____
_____
_____
_____

Structure
_____
_____
_____
_____

Name: _____ Date: _____

 **Activity**

Literature Web

Directions: Complete a Literature Web about the four *tanka* in *Desert Exile: The Uprooting of a Japanese American Family.*

Key Words
_____
_____
_____
_____
_____

Feelings
_____
_____
_____
_____
_____

Ideas
_____
_____
_____
_____
_____
_____

Title
_____
_____
_____
_____

Images/Symbols
_____
_____
_____
_____
_____
_____

Structure
_____
_____
_____

Name: _____ Date: _____

 **Activity**

Directions: Use the Hamburger Model to organize ideas for your essay responding to this prompt: *Could what happened to the Japanese Americans happen again to other groups in today's American society? Support your answer.*

**Introduction
(State your opinion.)**

_____

_____

Elaboration	**Elaboration**	**Elaboration**
_____	_____	_____
_____	_____	_____
_____	_____	_____
Reason	**Reason**	**Reason**
_____	_____	_____
_____	_____	_____
_____	_____	_____
Elaboration	**Elaboration**	**Elaboration**
_____	_____	_____
_____	_____	_____
_____	_____	_____

Conclusion

_____

_____

Activity

Characteristics of an Issue

Directions: Read and discuss the characteristics of an issue. Consider the difference between a topic and an issue. In the space provided, describe why the issue being discussed in class satisfies each characteristic of an issue.

- **Real world.** An issue is a controversy or problem that people are discussing or should be discussing. It is ambiguous with no clear-cut or easy solutions. As new information is obtained, the problem changes.

  _____

  _____

  _____

  _____

  _____

  _____

  _____

- **Multiple points of view.** Different people or groups have different points of view on an issue. Depending on how the issue is resolved, various individuals or groups (called stakeholders) stand to win or lose tangible things, such as income or recreational space, or intangible things, such as privacy or freedom of speech.

  _____

  _____

  _____

  _____

  _____

  _____

  _____

- **Researchable with substantial information available.** Remember that to develop a convincing argument, you will need multiple sources of information and data. Important issues and real-world problems are informed by historical and contemporary sources of information and by the collection and analysis of a variety of data.

_____

_____

_____

_____

_____

_____

- **Worthy topic and personal involvement.** Research offers the opportunity to ask questions about things that matter. While asking questions and seeking solutions, you have the chance to consider the arguments of others and to contribute your personal perspective and original thinking. When you care about an issue, you will be willing to spend time digging for evidence, taking a stand, developing an argument, and proposing a solution to the problem.

_____

_____

_____

_____

_____

Name: _____ Date: _____

Research Assignment

Directions: World War II served as a catalyst for dramatic changes in the United States and throughout the world. For example, women took on jobs formerly reserved for men; racism and human rights became global issues; and industrialization and new technologies changed economic, political, and social expectations. To understand the changes in these areas that are still occurring today, it is necessary first to understand the changes that occurred during the 1940s.

For the unit research project, you will investigate the impact of World War II on an aspect of life in the United States, such as the role of women, racism, human rights, industrialization, new technologies, or scientific discoveries. A list of suggested issues for research is given below the outline of the assignment requirements. If you want to research an issue that is not included on the list, discuss your idea with your teacher.

Requirements

- **Final product:** Write a paper (3–5 double-spaced pages with internal citations) and prepare and deliver a short oral presentation (3–5 minutes) sharing your findings with the class.

- **Lesson 15:** Complete your reading and interviews and gathering your evidence (Steps 1–4 on the Research Model Planner), and bring your resource materials and notes to class so that you can begin to plan your paper and presentation.

- **Lesson 18:** Prepare a draft of your paper for an in-class workshop.

- **Lesson 19:** Bring your draft of a paper, resource materials, and notes to class so that you can continue work on your paper and presentation.

- **Lesson 20:** Submit the final draft of your paper and deliver your oral presentation.

Suggested Research Issues

- What were the effects of changes in the participation of women in the workforce in the 1940s?

- Whom should the U.S. military have drafted during World War II?

- Should the United States have a period of mandatory military service?

- Should women in the U.S. military engage in combat?

- How did issues related to race affect the functioning of the U.S. military during World War II?

- Should the United States maintain nuclear weapons, and if so, under what conditions?

- Should the federal government spend money on the military in peacetime, and if so, under what conditions?

- What should happen to the military of a nation that has been defeated in war?

- Should restitution be made to the victims of a war? If so, what kind of restitution, and to which victims?

- Should war be covered live on television?

- What were the positive effects of technological changes in the 1940s? What were the negative effects?

- How should U.S. immigration policies restrict or encourage the immigration of persecuted groups from other countries?

Name: _____ Date: _____

Research Model Planner

Directions: Use this planner to guide you as you research your issue. Record your responses on another sheet of paper so that you have enough space for all your ideas.

1. Identify your issue or problem.

   • What is the issue or problem?

   _____

   _____

   _____

   • Who are the stakeholders and what are their positions?

   _____

   _____

   _____

   • What is my position on this issue?

   _____

   _____

   _____

2. Read about your issue and identify points of view or arguments through information sources.

   • What are my print sources?

   _____

   _____

   _____

• What are my media sources?

_____

_____

_____

• Who are my people sources?

_____

_____

_____

• What primary and secondary source documents might I use?

_____

_____

_____

• What are my preliminary findings based on a review of existing sources?

_____

_____

_____

3. Form a set of questions that can be answered by a specific set of data.

• What would be the results of _____ ?

_____

_____

_____

• Who would benefit and by how much?

_____

_____

_____

• Who would be harmed and by how much?

_____

_____

_____

• What are my research questions?

_____

_____

_____

4. Gather evidence through research techniques such as surveys, interviews, or analysis of primary and secondary source documents.

• What survey questions should I ask?

_____

_____

_____

• What interview questions should I ask?

_____

_____

_____

• What generalizations do secondary sources give?

_____

_____

_____

• What data and evidence can I find in primary sources to support different sides of the issue?

_____

_____

_____

5. Manipulate and transform data so that they can be interpreted.

• How can I summarize what I learned?

_____

_____

_____

• Should I develop charts, diagrams, or graphs to represent my data?

_____

_____

_____

6. Draw conclusions and make inferences.

• What do the data mean? How can I interpret what I found out?

_____

_____

_____

- How do the data support my original point of view?

_____

_____

_____

- How do they support other points of view?

_____

_____

_____

- What conclusions can I make about the issue?

_____

_____

_____

- What is my point of view now, based on the data?

_____

_____

_____

7. Determine implications and consequences.

- What could be the consequences of following the point of view that I support?

_____

_____

_____

- Do I know enough or are there now new questions to be answered?

_____

_____

_____

8. Communicate your findings. (Prepare a paper and oral presentation.)

- What are my purpose, issue, and point of view, and how will I explain them?

_____

_____

_____

- What data will I use to support my point of view?

_____

_____

_____

- How will I conclude my presentation?

_____

_____

Name: _____ Date: _____

Activity

Interview Planning Form

Directions: Respond to the following questions to help you plan your interview.

What is the name of person you will interview? _____

What is the role of this person? _____

Why do you want to interview this person? _____

_____

_____

_____

What will you tell this person about the issue you are researching? _____

_____

_____

_____

What questions will you ask? Consider adapting the following suggestions for your interview:

- *What is your perspective on the issue?*
- *How does the issue relate to your life or work?*
- *What sources would you consult if you were in my position?*

List the questions you will ask.

_____

_____

_____

_____

_____

_____

Name: _____ Date: _____

 **Activity**

Directions: Complete the chart for the issue being discussed in class.

Developing an Issue
State the issue: _____   _____   _____   _____   _____

Identify the stakeholder groups:	Describe the position of each group:
_____ _____ _____ _____ _____ _____ _____	_____ _____ _____ _____ _____ _____ _____

| State your initial position:

 _____

 _____

 _____

 _____

 _____ |

Name: _____ Date: _____

Developing an Issue

Directions: Complete the chart for a current issue related to science.

Developing an Issue

State the issue:

_____

_____

_____

_____

_____

Identify the stakeholder groups:	**Describe the position of each group:**
_____	_____
_____	_____
_____	_____
_____	_____
_____	_____
_____	_____
_____	_____

State your initial position:

_____

_____

_____

_____

_____

One Friday Morning

Langston Hughes

The thrilling news did not come directly to Nancy Lee, but it came in little indirections that finally added themselves up to one tremendous fact: she had won the prize! But being a calm and quiet young lady, she did not say anything, although the whole high school buzzed with rumors, guesses, reportedly authentic announcements on the part of students who had no right to be making announcements at all—since no student really knew yet who had won this year's art scholarship.

But Nancy Lee's drawing was so good, her lines so sure, her colors so bright and harmonious, that certainly no other student in the senior art class at George Washington High was thought to have very much of a chance. Yet you never could tell. Last year nobody had expected Joe Williams to win the Artist Club scholarship with that funny modernistic water color he had done of the high-level bridge. In fact, it was hard to make out there was a bridge until you had looked at the picture a long time. Still, Joe Williams got the prize, was feted by the community's leading painters, club women, and society folks at a big banquet at the Park-Rose Hotel, and was now an award student at the Art School—the city's only art school.

Nancy Lee Johnson was a colored girl, a few years out of the South. But seldom did her high-school classmates think of her as colored. She was smart, pretty, and brown, and fitted in well with the life of the school. She stood high in scholarship, played a swell game of basketball, had taken part in the senior musical in a soft, velvety voice, and had never seemed to intrude or stand out, except in pleasant ways, so it was seldom even mentioned—her color.

Nancy Lee sometimes forgot she was colored herself. She liked her classmates and her school. Particularly she liked her art teacher, Miss Dietrich, the tall red-haired woman who taught her law and order in doing things; and the beauty of working step by step until a job is done; a picture finished; a design created; or a block print carved out of nothing but an idea and a smooth square of linoleum, inked, proofs made, and finally put down on paper—clean, sharp, beautiful, individual, unlike any other in the world, thus making the paper have a meaning nobody else could give it except Nancy Lee. That was the wonderful thing about true creation. You made something nobody else on earth could make—but you.

Miss Dietrich was the kind of teacher who brought out the best in her students—but their own best, not anybody else's copied best. For anybody else's best, great though it might be, even Michelangelo's, wasn't enough to please Miss Dietrich, dealing with the creative impulses of young men and women living in an American city in the Middle West, and being American.

Nancy Lee was proud of being American, a Negro American with blood out of Africa a long time ago, too many generations back to count. But her parents had taught her the beauties of Africa, its strength, its song, its mighty rivers, its early smelting of iron, its building of the pyramids, and its ancient and important civilizations. And Miss Dietrich had discovered for her the sharp and humorous lines of African sculpture, Benin, Congo, Makonde. Nancy Lee's father was a mail carrier, her mother a social worker in a city settlement house. Both parents had been to Negro colleges in the South. And her mother had gotten a further degree in social work from a Northern university. Her parents were, like most Americans, simple, ordinary people who had worked hard and steadily for their education. Now they were trying to make it easier for Nancy Lee to achieve learning than it had been for them. They would be very happy when they heard of the award to their daughter—yet Nancy did not tell them. To surprise them would be better. Besides, there had been a promise.

Casually, one day, Miss Dietrich asked Nancy Lee what color frame she thought would be best on her picture. That had been the first inkling.

"Blue," Nancy Lee said. Although the picture had been entered in the Artist Club contest a month ago, Nancy Lee did not hesitate in her choice of a color for the possible frame, since she could still see her picture clearly in her mind's eye—for that picture waiting for the blue frame had come out of her soul, her own life, and had bloomed into miraculous being with Miss Dietrich's help. It was, she knew, the best water color she had painted in her four years as a high-school art student, and she was glad she had made something Miss Dietrich liked well enough to permit her to enter in the contest before she graduated.

It was not a modernistic picture in the sense that you had to look at it a long time to understand what it meant. It was just a simple scene in the city park on a spring day, with the trees still leaflessly lacy against the sky, the new grass fresh and green, a flag on a tall pole in the center, children playing, and an old Negro woman sitting on a bench with her head turned. A lot for one picture, to be sure, but it was not there in heavy and final detail like a calendar. Its charm was that everything was light and airy, happy like spring, with a lot of blue sky, paper-white clouds, and air showing through. You could tell that the old Negro woman was looking at the flag, and that the flag was proud in the spring breeze, and that the breeze helped to make the children's dresses billow as they played.

Miss Dietrich had taught Nancy Lee how to paint spring, people, and a breeze on what was only a plain white piece of paper from the supply closet. But Miss Dietrich had not said make it like any other spring-people-breeze ever seen before. She let it remain Nancy Lee's own. That is how the old Negro woman happened to be there looking at the flag—for in her mind the flag, the spring, and the woman formed a kind of triangle holding a dream Nancy Lee wanted to express. White stars on a blue field, spring, children, ever-growing life, and an old woman. Would the judges at the Artist Club like it?

One wet, rainy April afternoon Miss O'Shay, the girls' vice-principal, sent for Nancy Lee to stop by her office as school closed. Pupils without umbrellas or raincoats were clustered in doorways, hoping to make it home between showers. Outside the skies were gray. Nancy Lee's thoughts were suddenly gray, too.

She did not think she had done anything wrong, yet that tight little knot came in her throat just the same as she approached Miss O'Shay's door. Perhaps she had banged her locker too often and too hard. Perhaps the note in French she had written to Sallie halfway across the study hall just for fun had never gotten to Sallie but into Miss O'Shay's hands instead. Or maybe she was failing in some subject and wouldn't be allowed to graduate. Chemistry! A pang went through the pit of her stomach.

She knocked on Miss O'Shay's door. That familiarly solid and competent voice said, "Come in."

Miss O'Shay had a way of making you feel welcome, even if you came to be expelled.

"Sit down, Nancy Lee Johnson," said Miss O'Shay. "I have something to tell you." Nancy Lee sat down. "But I must ask you to promise not to tell anyone yet."

"I won't, Miss O'Shay," Nancy Lee said, wondering what on earth the principal had to say to her.

"You are about to graduate," Miss O'Shay said. "And we shall miss you. You have been an excellent student, Nancy, and you will not be without honors on the senior list, as I am sure you know."

At that point there was a light knock on the door. Miss O'Shay called out, "Come in," and Miss Dietrich entered. "May I be a part of this, too?" she asked, tall and smiling.

"Of course," Miss O'Shay said. "I was just telling Nancy Lee what we thought of her. But I hadn't gotten around to giving her the news. Perhaps, Miss Dietrich, you'd like to tell her yourself."

Miss Dietrich was always direct. "Nancy Lee," she said, "your picture has won the Artist Club scholarship."

The slender brown girl's eyes widened, her heart jumped, then her throat tightened again. She tried to smile, but instead tears came to her eyes.

"Dear Nancy Lee," Miss O'Shay said, "we are so happy for you." The elderly white woman took her hand and shook it warmly while Miss Dietrich beamed with pride.

Nancy Lee must have danced all the way home. She never remembered quite how she got there through the rain. She hoped she had been dignified. But certainly she hadn't stopped to tell anybody her secret on the way. Raindrops, smiles, and tears mingled on her brown cheeks. She hoped her mother hadn't yet gotten home and that the house was empty. She wanted to have time to calm down and look natural before she had to see anyone. She didn't want to be bursting with excitement—having a secret to contain.

Miss O'Shay's calling her to the office had been in the nature of a preparation and a warning. The kind, elderly vice-principal said she did not believe in catching young ladies unawares, even with honors, so she wished her to know about the coming award. In making acceptance speeches she wanted her to be calm, prepared, not nervous, overcome, and frightened. So Nancy Lee was asked to think what she would say when the scholarship was conferred upon her a few days hence, both at the Friday morning high-school assembly hour, when the announcement would be made, and at the evening banquet of the Artist Club.

Nancy Lee promised the vice-principal to think calmly about what she would say.

Miss Dietrich had then asked for some facts about her parents, her background, and her life, since such material would probably be desired for the papers. Nancy Lee had told her how, six years before, they had come up from the Deep South, her father having been successful in achieving a transfer from the one post office to another, a thing he had long sought in order to give Nancy Lee a chance to go to school in the North. Now they lived in a modest Negro neighborhood, went to see the best plays when they came to town, and had been saving to send Nancy Lee to art school, in case she were permitted to enter. But the scholarship would help a great deal, for they were not rich people.

"Now Mother can have a new coat next winter," Nancy Lee thought, "because my tuition will all be covered for the first year. And once in art school, there are other scholarships I can win."

Dreams began to dance through her head, plans and ambitions, beauties she would create for herself, her parents, and the Negro people—for Nancy Lee possessed a deep and reverent race pride. She could see the old woman in her picture (really her grandmother in the South) lifting her head to the bright stars on the flag in the distance. A Negro in America! Often hurt, discriminated against, sometimes lynched—but always there were the stars on the blue body of the flag. Was there any other flag in the world that had so many stars? Nancy Lee thought deeply, but she could remember none in all the encyclopedias or geographies she had ever looked into.

"Hitch your wagon to a star," Nancy Lee thought, dancing home in the rain. "Who were our flag-makers?"

Friday morning came, the morning when the world would know—her high-school world, the newspaper world, her mother and dad. Dad could not be there at the assembly to hear the announcement, nor see her prize picture displayed on the stage, nor listen to Nancy Lee's little speech of acceptance, but Mother would be able to come, although Mother was much puzzled as to why Nancy Lee was so insistent she be at school on that particular Friday morning.

When something is happening, something new and fine, something that will change your very life, it is hard to go to sleep at night for thinking about it, and hard to keep your heart from pounding, or a strange little knot of joy from gathering in your throat. Nancy Lee had taken her bath, brushed her hair until it glowed, and had gone to bed thinking about the next day, the big day, when before three thousand students, she would be the one student honored, her painting the one painting to be acclaimed as the best of the year from all the art classes of the city. Her short speech of gratitude was ready. She went over it in her mind, not word for word (because she didn't want it to sound as if she had learned it by heart), but she let the thoughts flow simply and sincerely through her consciousness many times.

When the president of the Artist Club presented her with the medal and scroll of the scholarship award, she would say:

"Judges and members of the Artist Club. I want to thank you for this award that means so much to me personally and through me to my people, the colored people of this city, who, sometimes, are discouraged and bewildered, thinking that color and poverty are against them. I accept this award with gratitude and pride, not for myself alone, but for my race that believes in American opportunity and American fairness—and the bright stars in our flag. I thank Miss Dietrich and the teachers who made it possible for me to have the knowledge and training that lie behind this honor you have conferred upon my painting. When I came here from the South a few years ago, I was not sure how you would receive me. You received me well. You have given me a chance and helped me along the road I wanted to follow. I suppose the judges know that every week here at assembly the students of this school pledge allegiance to the flag. I shall try to be worthy of that pledge, and of the help and friendship and understanding of my fellow citizens of whatever race or creed, and of our American dream of 'Liberty and justice for all!'"

That would be her response before the students in the morning. How proud and happy the Negro pupils would be, perhaps almost as proud as they were of the one colored star on the football team. Her mother would probably cry with happiness. Thus Nancy Lee went to sleep dreaming of a wonderful tomorrow.

The bright sunlight of an April morning woke her. There was breakfast with her parents—their half-amused and puzzled faces across the table, wondering what could be this secret that made her eyes so bright. The swift walk to school; the clock in the tower almost nine; hundreds of pupils streaming into the long, rambling old building that was the city's largest high school; the sudden quiet of the homeroom after the bell rang; then the teacher opening her record book to call the roll. But just before she began, she looked across the room until her eyes located Nancy Lee.

"Nancy," she said, "Miss O'Shay would like to see you in her office, please."

Nancy Lee rose and went out while the names were being called and the word *present* added its period to each name.

Perhaps, Nancy Lee thought, the reporters from the papers had already come. Maybe they wanted to take her picture before assembly, which wasn't until ten o'clock. (Last year they had had the photograph of the winner of the award in the morning papers as soon as the announcement had been made.)

Nancy Lee knocked at Miss O'Shay's door.

"Come in."

The vice-principal stood at her desk. There was no one else in the room. It was very quiet.

"Sit down, Nancy Lee," she said. Miss O'Shay did not smile. There was a long pause. The seconds went by slowly. "I do not know how to tell you what I have to say," the elderly woman began, her eyes on the papers on her desk. "I am indignant and ashamed for myself and for this city." Then she lifted her eyes and looked at Nancy Lee in the neat blue dress, sitting there before her. "You are not to receive the scholarship this morning."

Outside in the hail the electric bells announcing the first period rang, loud and interminably long. Miss O'Shay remained silent. To the brown girl there in the chair, the room grew suddenly smaller, smaller, smaller, and there was no air. She could not speak.

Miss O'Shay said, "When the committee learned that you were colored, they changed their plans."

Still Nancy Lee said nothing, for there was no air to give breath to her lungs.

"Here is the letter from the committee, Nancy Lee." Miss O'Shay picked it up and read the final paragraph to her.

"It seems to us wiser to arbitrarily rotate the award among the various high schools of the city from now on. And especially in this case since the student chosen happens to be colored, a circumstance which unfortunately, had we known, might have prevented this embarrassment. But there have never been any Negro students in the local art school, and the presence of one there might create difficulties for all concerned. We have high regard for the quality of Nancy Lee Johnson's talent, but we do not feel it would be fair to honor it with the Artist Club award." Miss O'Shay paused. She put the letter down.

"Nancy Lee, I am very sorry to have to give you this message."

"But my speech," Nancy Lee said, "was about …" The words stuck in her throat. "… about America. …"

Miss O'Shay had risen; she turned her back and stood looking out the window at the spring tulips in the school yard.

"I thought, since the award would be made at assembly right after our oath of allegiance," the words tumbled almost hysterically from Nancy Lee's throat now, "I would put part of the flag salute in my speech. You know, Miss O'Shay, that part about liberty and justice for all."

"I know," said Miss O'Shay, slowly facing the room again. "But America is only what we who believe in it make it. I am Irish. You may not know, Nancy Lee, but years ago we were called the dirty Irish, and mobs rioted against us in the big cities, and we were invited to go back where we came from. But we didn't go. And we didn't give up, because we believed in the American dream, and in our power to make that dream come true. Difficulties, yes. Mountains to climb, yes. Discouragements to face, yes. Democracy to *make,* yes. That is it, Nancy Lee! We still have in this world of ours democracy to make. You and I, Nancy Lee. But the premise and the base are here, the lines of the Declaration of Independence and the words of Lincoln are here, and the stars in our flag. Those who deny you this scholarship do not know the meaning of those stars, but it's up to us to make them know. As a teacher in the public schools of this city, I myself will go before

the school board and ask them to remove from our system the offer of any prizes or awards denied to any student because of race or color."

Suddenly Miss O'Shay stopped speaking. Her clear, clear blue eyes looked into those of the girl before her. The woman's eyes were full of strength and courage. "Lift up your head, Nancy Lee, and smile at me."

Miss O'Shay stood against the open window with the green lawn and the tulips beyond, the sunlight tangled in her gray hair, her voice an electric flow of strength to the hurt spirit of Nancy Lee. The Abolitionists who believed in freedom when there was slavery must have been like that. The first white teachers who went into the Deep South to teach the freed slaves must have been like that. All those who stand against ignorance, narrowness, hate, and mud on stars must be like that.

Nancy Lee lifted her head and smiled. The bell for assembly rang. She went through the long hail filled with students, toward the auditorium.

"There will be other awards," Nancy Lee thought. "There're schools in other cities. This won't keep me down. But when I'm a woman, I'll fight to see that these things don't happen to other girls as this has happened to me. And men and women like Miss O'Shay will help me."

She took her seat among the seniors. The doors of the auditorium closed. As the principal came onto the platform, the students rose and turned their eyes to the flag on the stage.

One hand went to the heart, the other outstretched toward the flag. Three thousand voices spoke. Among them was the voice of a dark girl whose cheeks were suddenly wet with tears, "… one nation indivisible, with liberty and justice for all."

"That is the land we must make," she thought.

Name: _____ Date: _____

Activity

Literature Web

Directions: Complete the Literature Web for "One Friday Morning."

Key Words	Feelings
_____	_____
_____	_____
_____	_____
_____	_____
_____	_____

Ideas	Title	Images/Symbols
_____	_____	_____
_____	_____	_____
_____	_____	_____
_____	_____	_____
_____		_____
_____		_____

Structure

_____

_____

_____

_____

Name: _____ Date: _____

 **Activity**

Directions: Complete the Vocabulary Web for the word assigned to you.

Word Families
_____
_____
_____
_____
_____
_____

Synonyms
_____
_____

Antonyms
_____
_____

Dictionary Definition
_____
_____

Word
_____

Analysis

Part of Speech
_____

Origin
_____
_____
_____

Sentence in Text
_____
_____
_____
_____

Stems
_____
_____
_____

Student Example
_____
_____

Activity
12A

Comparisons Across Time: Literature

Directions: Compare selected works of literature from the 1940s with contemporary works of literature.

Work from the 1940s	Contemporary Work

Name: _____ Date: _____

 **Activity**
12B

Directions: Compare selected pieces of music from the 1940s with contemporary pieces of music.

Pieces from the 1940s	Contemporary Piece

Name: _____ Date: _____

Comparisons Across Time: Art

Directions: Compare selected works of art from the 1940s with contemporary works of art.

Work from the 1940s	Contemporary Work

Name: _____ Date: _____

 **Activity**

Directions: Complete the Art Web for a work of art created in the 1940s.

Description of the Work

_____

_____

_____

_____

_____

_____

Feelings

_____

_____

_____

_____

_____

_____

Ideas

_____

_____

_____

_____

_____

_____

_____

Title

_____

_____

_____

_____

Images/Symbols

_____

_____

_____

_____

_____

_____

_____

Form

_____

_____

_____

_____

Activity

Reflections of National and World Events in Popular Culture

Directions: Consider how the examples of popular culture that you are examining reflect the broader events and concerns of the 1940s. Use the chart to organize your thoughts.

Example/Aspect of the Popular Culture of the 1940s	National and World Events Reflected in the Popular Culture

Name: _____ Date: _____

Vocabulary Web

Directions: Complete the Vocabulary Web for *genocide.*

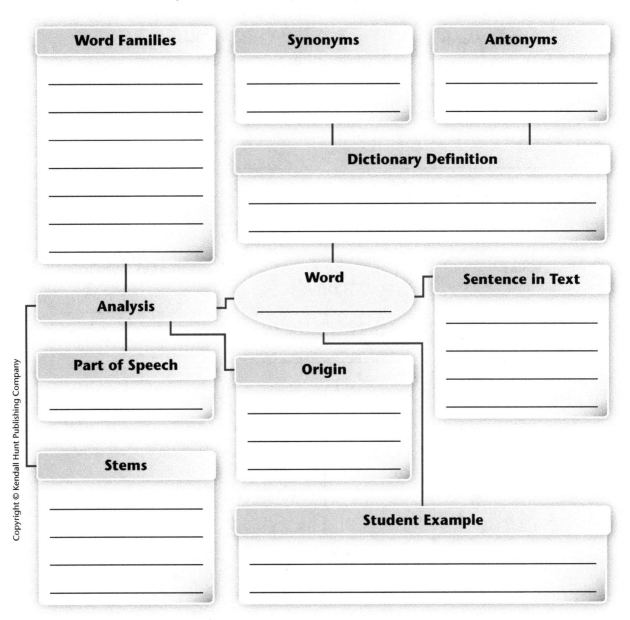

| Word Families | Synonyms | Antonyms |

| Dictionary Definition |

Word

| Analysis | Sentence in Text |

| Part of Speech | Origin |

| Stems |

| Student Example |

Copyright © Kendall Hunt Publishing Company

Name: _____ Date: _____

 **Activity**

Directions: Complete the Literature Web for a section of *The Member of the Wedding.*

Key Words	Feelings
_____	_____
_____	_____
_____	_____
_____	_____
_____	_____

Ideas

_____
_____
_____
_____
_____
_____

Title

_____
_____
_____
_____

Images/Symbols

_____
_____
_____
_____
_____
_____

Structure

_____
_____
_____
_____

Name: _____ Date: _____

Vocabulary Web

Directions: Complete the Vocabulary Web for a word of your choice from *The Member of the Wedding.*

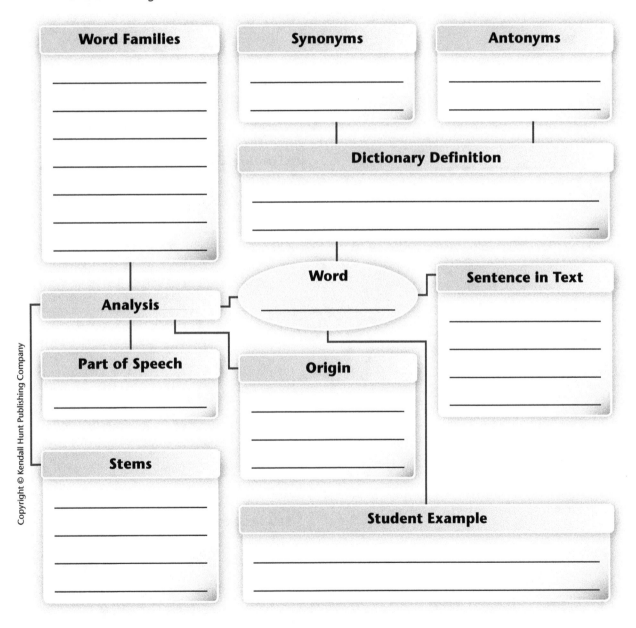

Name: _____ Date: _____

 **Activity**

Directions: Complete the Vocabulary Web for a word of your choice from *The Member of the Wedding.*

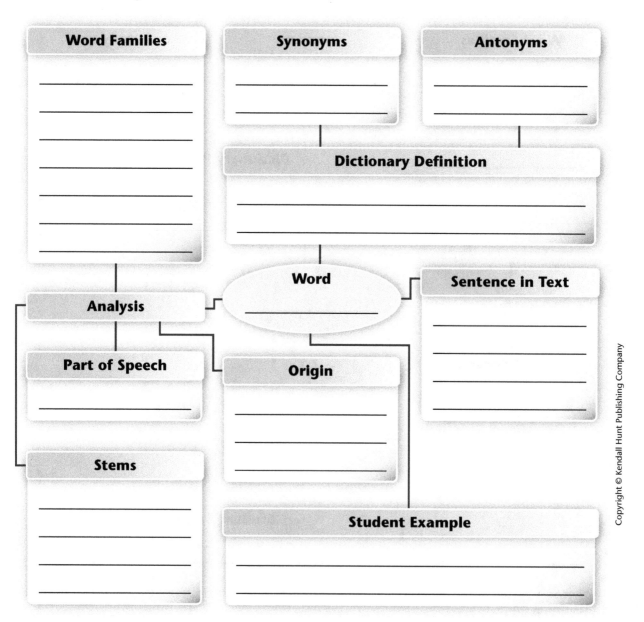

Word Families

_____
_____
_____
_____
_____

Synonyms

_____
_____

Antonyms

_____
_____

Dictionary Definition

_____
_____

Word

_____

Analysis

Part of Speech

_____

Stems

_____
_____

Origin

_____
_____

Sentence in Text

_____
_____
_____

Student Example

_____
_____

Name: _____ Date: _____

Literature Web

Directions: Complete the Literature Web for a section of *Hiroshima*.

Key Words
_____
_____
_____
_____
_____
_____

Feelings
_____
_____
_____
_____
_____
_____

Ideas
_____
_____
_____
_____
_____
_____

Title
_____
_____
_____
_____

Images/Symbols
_____
_____
_____
_____
_____
_____

Structure
_____
_____
_____
_____

Name: _____ Date: _____

 **Activity**

Directions: Complete the Vocabulary Web for a word of your choice from *Hiroshima.*

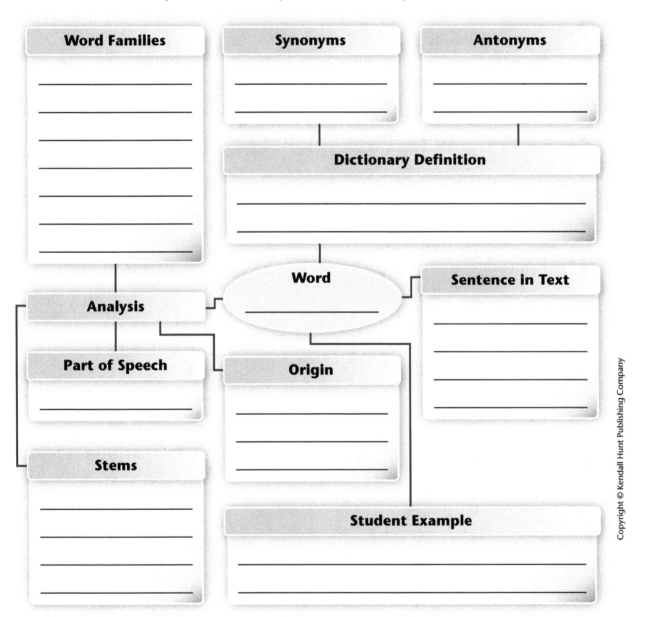

Word Families

_____
_____
_____
_____
_____
_____

Synonyms

_____
_____

Antonyms

_____
_____

Dictionary Definition

_____
_____

Word

_____

Analysis

Part of Speech

_____

Origin

_____
_____

Sentence in Text

_____
_____
_____

Stems

_____
_____

Student Example

_____
_____

Activity

Vocabulary Web

Directions: Complete the Vocabulary Web for a word of your choice from *Hiroshima*.

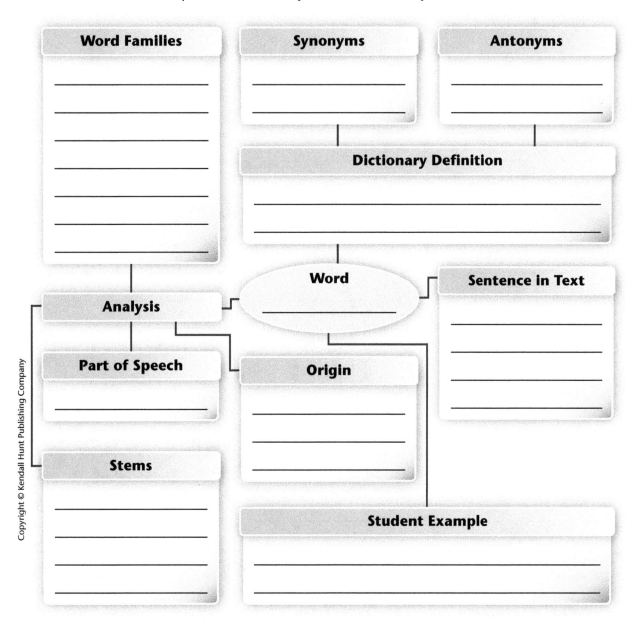

Word Families	Synonyms	Antonyms

Dictionary Definition

Word

Analysis

Sentence in Text

Part of Speech

Origin

Stems

Student Example

Name: _____ Date: _____

 **Activity**

Directions: Use the Hamburger Model to plan a persuasive essay arguing for the importance of making efforts to record the oral histories of individuals. Draft your essay on a separate sheet of paper.

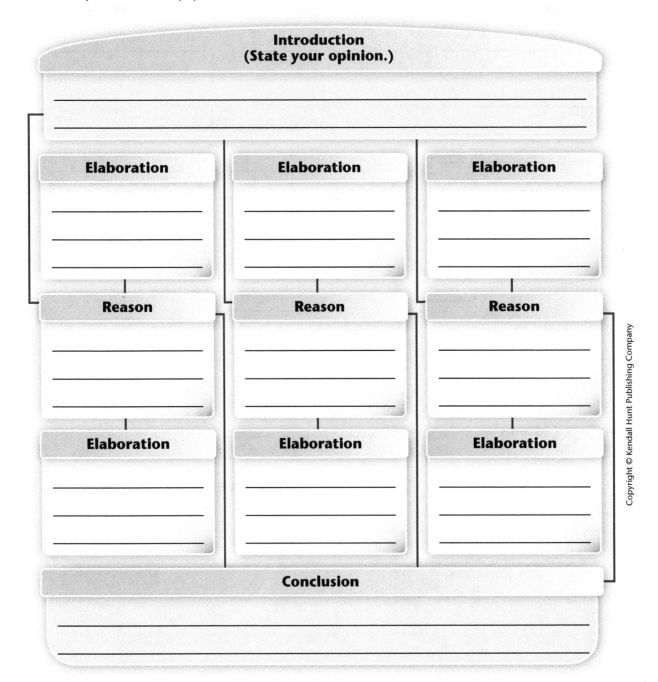

**Introduction
(State your opinion.)**

Elaboration

Elaboration

Elaboration

Reason

Reason

Reason

Elaboration

Elaboration

Elaboration

Conclusion

Name: _____ Date: _____

Activity

Directions: Evaluate the argument in "Address Unknown" by responding to the questions. Give examples to support your responses.

1. **Clarity:** Would anyone who reads the selection be able to understand its argument? Are the reasons clear? Are they explained thoroughly, or is more information needed?

_____

_____

_____

2. **Accuracy:** Is the supporting evidence factual and correct?

_____

_____

_____

3. **Precision:** Are the reasons and evidence specific, or are they general and vague?

_____

_____

_____

4. **Relevance:** How are the reasons and evidence connected to the question? Is the information important to the issue?

_____

_____

_____

Adapted from Paul, R. (1992). *Critical thinking: What every person needs to know to survive in a rapidly changing world.* Sonoma, CA: Foundation for Critical Thinking.

5. **Depth:** How does the author address the complexities raised by the question? Are the arguments and reasons strong and important, or do they seem superficial?

_____

_____

_____

6. **Breadth:** Are enough different reasons given to make the argument convincing? Are different points of view presented? Is there another way to look at this question?

_____

_____

_____

7. **Logic:** Is the argument logical? Do the sentences seem to go together, and does their sequence make sense? Or does the selection sound like a set of disconnected statements?

_____

_____

_____

Copyright © Kendall Hunt Publishing Company

Name: _____ Date: _____

Activity

Developing an Issue

Directions: Select an issue which resulted in a verbal apology or financial restitution being made. Complete the chart for this issue.

Developing an Issue
State the issue: _____   _____   _____   _____

Identify the stakeholder groups:	Describe the position of each group:
_____ _____ _____ _____ _____ _____	_____ _____ _____ _____ _____ _____

State your initial position: _____   _____   _____   _____   _____

Name: _____ Date: _____

Activity

Directions: Use the Hamburger Model to plan a paragraph stating your position on an issue which resulted in a verbal apology or financial restitution being made. Draft your paragraph on a separate sheet of paper.

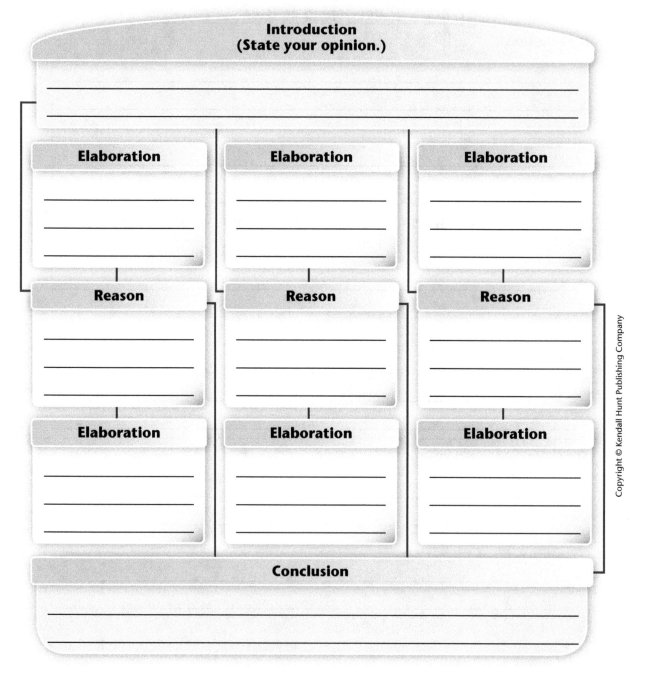

**Introduction
(State your opinion.)**

_____

_____

Elaboration	**Elaboration**	**Elaboration**
_____ _____ _____	_____ _____ _____	_____ _____ _____
Reason	**Reason**	**Reason**
_____ _____ _____	_____ _____ _____	_____ _____ _____
Elaboration	**Elaboration**	**Elaboration**
_____ _____ _____	_____ _____ _____	_____ _____ _____

Conclusion

_____

_____

Name: _____ Date: _____

Vocabulary Web

Directions: Complete the Vocabulary Web for the word assigned to you.

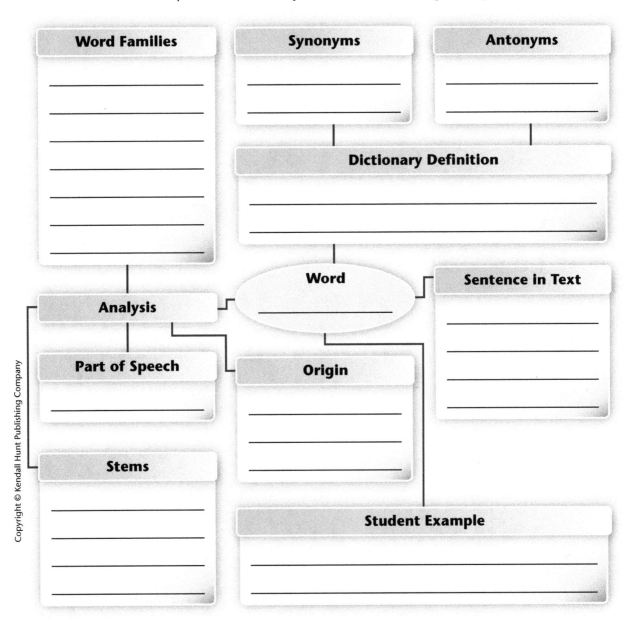

Word Families
_____
_____
_____
_____
_____
_____

Synonyms
_____
_____

Antonyms
_____
_____

Dictionary Definition
_____
_____

Word
_____

Analysis

Part of Speech
_____

Origin
_____
_____
_____

Sentence in Text
_____
_____
_____
_____

Stems
_____
_____
_____

Student Example
_____
_____

Name: _____ Date: _____

Oral Presentation Evaluation Form

Assignment: _____

Directions: For 1–10, circle the choice that best describes your presentation. Then complete the two sentences.

Content

1. The purpose of the presentation was clear.

   Needs improvement   Satisfactory   Excellent

2. I included details that supported the main idea.

   Needs improvement   Satisfactory   Excellent

3. I showed knowledge of the subject.

   Needs improvement   Satisfactory   Excellent

4. I used vocabulary that was rich, varied, and persuasive.

   Needs improvement   Satisfactory   Excellent

Organization

5. The structure clearly followed the Hamburger Model (introduction, body, conclusion).

   Needs improvement   Satisfactory   Excellent

6. The ideas flowed smoothly and in an orderly way.

   Needs improvement   Satisfactory   Excellent

7. I closed the presentation with a strong, interesting idea that restated the purpose.

   Needs improvement   Satisfactory   Excellent

Delivery

8. I made good eye contact with the audience.

Needs improvement   Satisfactory   Excellent

9. The volume of my presentation was adequate.

Needs improvement   Satisfactory   Excellent

10. I spoke clearly and could be understood.

Needs improvement   Satisfactory   Excellent

The best part of my presentation was:

_____

_____

_____

One way I could improve is:

_____

_____

_____

Name: _____ Date: _____

Oral Presentation Evaluation Form

Activity

Speaker: _____ **Assignment:** _____

Directions: For 1–10, circle the choice that best describes the presentation you are evaluating. Then complete the two sentences.

Content

1. The purpose of the presentation was clear.

   Needs improvement   Satisfactory   Excellent

2. The speech included details that supported the main idea.

   Needs improvement   Satisfactory   Excellent

3. The speaker showed knowledge of the subject.

   Needs improvement   Satisfactory   Excellent

4. The speaker used vocabulary that was rich, varied, and persuasive.

   Needs improvement   Satisfactory   Excellent

Organization

5. The structure clearly followed the Hamburger Model (introduction, body, conclusion).

   Needs improvement   Satisfactory   Excellent

6. The ideas flowed smoothly and in an orderly way.

   Needs improvement   Satisfactory   Excellent

7. The speech concluded with a strong, interesting idea that restated the purpose.

   Needs improvement   Satisfactory   Excellent

Delivery

8. The speaker made good eye contact with the audience and/or camera.

Needs improvement   Satisfactory   Excellent

9. The volume of the speech was adequate.

Needs improvement   Satisfactory   Excellent

10. The speaker spoke clearly and could be understood.

Needs improvement   Satisfactory   Excellent

The best part of this presentation was:

_____

_____

_____

_____

A suggestion for improvement is:

_____

_____

_____

_____

I Have a Rendezvous with Death

Alan Seeger

I have a rendezvous with Death
At some disputed barricade,
When Spring comes back with rustling shade
And apple-blossoms fill the air—
I have a rendezvous with Death
When Spring brings back blue days and fair.

It may be he shall take my hand
And lead me into his dark land
And close my eyes and quench my breath—
It may be I shall pass him still.
I have a rendezvous with Death
On some scarred slope of battered hill
When Spring comes round again this year
And the first meadow-flowers appear.

God knows 'twere better to be deep
Pillowed in silk and scented down,
Where love throbs out in blissful sleep,
Pulse nigh to pulse, and breath to breath,
Where hushed awakenings are dear …
But I've a rendezvous with Death
At midnight in some flaming town,
When Spring trips north again this year,
And I to my pledged word am true,
I shall not fail that rendezvous.

Murmurings in a Field Hospital

Carl Sandburg

*[They picked him up in the grass where he had lain two days
in the rain with a piece of shrapnel in his lungs.]*

Come to me only with playthings now …
A picture of a singing woman with blue eyes
Standing at a fence of hollyhocks, poppies and sunflowers …
Or an old man I remember sitting with children telling stories
Of days that never happened anywhere in the world …

No more iron cold and real to handle,
Shaped for a drive straight ahead.
Bring me only beautiful useless things.
Only old home things touched at sunset in the quiet …
And at the window one day in summer
Yellow of the new crock of butter
Stood against the red of new climbing roses …
And the world was all playthings.

Moratorium

Private John Lawrence Sheehan

Along with the letter, keys and such, I'll leave
My thoughts: civilian thoughts that cannot march
To military bands, that cannot breathe
In gas masks. Stored away with shirts in starch
And books in boxes, labeled neatly, rest
My restless thoughts. Assorted memories
Of certain plans, ignited and suppressed
Like fireflies. Love, a pollen on the breeze,
Inhaled on hilltops, suddenly, till breath
Had tiptoed with a shiver, and the world
Was windswept. Now inevitable Death
Or Victory advance. Our flag's unfurled.
Until the wars are won and treaties made,
I'll leave you here, my thoughts, where peace has stayed.

"Moratorium": From *Lines of Battle,* edited by Annette Tapert, Alfred A. Knopf Publishers.

World War II

Langston Hughes

What a grand time was the war!
  Oh, my, my!
What a grand time was the war!
  My, my, my!

In wartime we had fun,
Sorry that old war is done!
What a grand time was the war,
  My, my!

Echo:
  Did
  Somebody
  Die?

Name: _____ Date: _____

Poetry Analysis Form

Directions: Reread each of the two poems you selected. Take note of the key words and images in each poem as well as the thoughts, ideas, and questions you have in response to it. For each poem, respond to the prompts that follow.

Poem 1 (title): _____

1. Which phrase, sentence, or stanza is most interesting or effective to you? Explain its meaning and tell why you find it interesting or effective.

   _____

   _____

   _____

2. Write a new title for the poem. Give reasons from the poem that show why your new title is a good one.

   _____

   _____

   _____

3. Give examples of how the poet uses language and poetic devices to convey the meaning of the poem.

   _____

   _____

   _____

4. In what ways is the poem like others you have read in this unit? In what ways is it different?

   _____

   _____

   _____

Poem 2 (title): _____

1. Which phrase, sentence, or stanza is most interesting or effective to you? Explain its meaning and tell why you find it interesting or effective.

   _____

   _____

   _____

2. Write a new title for the poem. Give reasons from the poem that show why your new title is a good one.

   _____

   _____

   _____

3. Give examples of how the poet uses language and poetic devices to convey the meaning of the poem.

   _____

   _____

   _____

4. In what ways is the poem like others you have read in this unit? In what ways is it different?

   _____

   _____

   _____

Name: _____ Date: _____

Vocabulary Web

Directions: Complete the Vocabulary Web for the word assigned to you.

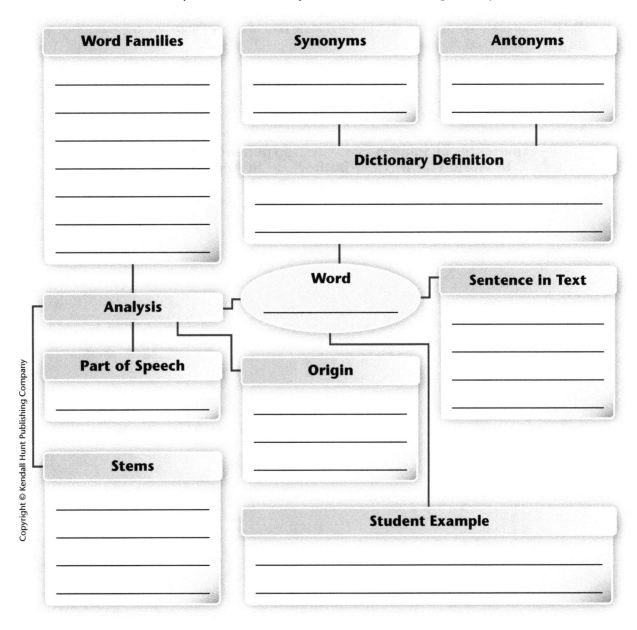

Word Families

Synonyms

Antonyms

Dictionary Definition

Analysis

Word

Sentence in Text

Part of Speech

Origin

Stems

Student Example

Name: _____ Date: _____

 **Activity**

Directions: Investigate the experiences of soldiers in another war. Use the Venn diagram to compare and contrast these experiences with those of soldiers who fought in World War II. Write the ways they are alike in the middle part of the diagram and the ways they are different in the outer parts.

**Experiences of Soldiers
in World War II**   **Both**   **Experiences of Soldiers
in Another War**

Name: _____ Date: _____

Compare and Contrast
Frankie Addams and Anne Frank

Activity

Directions: Use the Venn diagram to compare and contrast the ways that Frankie Addams and Anne Frank experience adolescence. Write the ways their experiences are alike in the middle part of the diagram and the ways they are different in the outer parts.

Frankie Addams   **Both**   **Anne Frank**

Name: _____ Date: _____

Stories from the 1940s

Directions: Use the chart to take notes on the class discussion about similarities and differences between the interviewees' experiences in the 1940s. In the left column, list common experiences. In the right column, list experiences that were unique to just one or two of the interviewees.

Common Experiences in the 1940s	Unique Experiences in the 1940s

Name: _____ Date: _____

 **Activity**

Directions: List three examples that illustrate each of the generalizations about change.

Change

> **Change is linked to time.**
> _____
> _____
> _____

> **Change is everywhere.**
> _____
> _____
> _____

> **Change may be positive or negative.**
> _____
> _____
> _____

> **Change may be perceived as orderly or random.**
> _____
> _____
> _____

> **Change may happen naturally or may be caused by people.**
> _____
> _____
> _____

Name: _____ Date: _____

Self-Review of Writing

Assignment: _____

Directions: Review your writing carefully. For each sentence, circle the choice that best describes your writing. Then complete the two sentences.

1. My main idea is clear.

    Needs improvement   Satisfactory   Excellent

2. My details support the main idea.

    Needs improvement   Satisfactory   Excellent

3. My ideas flow smoothly and in an orderly way.

    Needs improvement   Satisfactory   Excellent

4. The structure clearly follows the Hamburger Model (introduction, body, conclusion).

    Needs improvement   Satisfactory   Excellent

5. My vocabulary is rich and varied.

    Needs improvement   Satisfactory   Excellent

My writing is strong in these ways:

_____

_____

_____

My writing could be improved in these ways:

_____

_____

_____

Name: _____ Date: _____

 **Activity**
18D

Writer: _____ **Assignment:** _____

Directions: Read your partner's writing carefully. For each sentence, circle the choice that best describes the writing. Then complete the two sentences.

1. The main idea is clear.

   Needs improvement   Satisfactory   Excellent

2. The details support the main idea.

   Needs improvement   Satisfactory   Excellent

3. The ideas flow smoothly and in an orderly way.

   Needs improvement   Satisfactory   Excellent

4. The structure clearly follows the Hamburger Model (introduction, body, conclusion).

   Needs improvement   Satisfactory   Excellent

5. The vocabulary is rich and varied.

   Needs improvement   Satisfactory   Excellent

The writing is strong in these ways:

_____

_____

_____

The writing could be improved in these ways:

_____

_____

_____

Name: _____ Date: _____

Hamburger Model: Using the Atomic Bomb to End the War

Activity

Directions: Use the Hamburger Model to plan a persuasive essay explaining your perspective on the bombing of Hiroshima and Nagasaki at the conclusion of World War II. Draft your essay on a separate sheet of paper.

**Introduction
(State your opinion.)**

_____
_____

Elaboration	**Elaboration**	**Elaboration**
_____	_____	_____
_____	_____	_____
_____	_____	_____
Reason	**Reason**	**Reason**
_____	_____	_____
_____	_____	_____
_____	_____	_____
Elaboration	**Elaboration**	**Elaboration**
_____	_____	_____
_____	_____	_____
_____	_____	_____

Conclusion

_____
_____

Name: _____ Date: _____

Oral Presentation Evaluation Form

Speaker: _____ **Assignment:** _____

Directions: For 1–10, circle the choice that best describes the presentation. Then complete the two sentences.

Content

1. The purpose of the presentation was clear.

   Needs improvement   Satisfactory   Excellent

2. The speaker included details that supported the main idea.

   Needs improvement   Satisfactory   Excellent

3. The speaker showed knowledge of the subject.

   Needs improvement   Satisfactory   Excellent

4. The speaker used vocabulary that was rich, varied, and persuasive.

   Needs improvement   Satisfactory   Excellent

Organization

5. The structure clearly followed the Hamburger Model (introduction, body, conclusion).

   Needs improvement   Satisfactory   Excellent

6. The ideas flowed smoothly and in an orderly way.

   Needs improvement   Satisfactory   Excellent

7. The speaker closed the presentation with a strong, interesting idea that restated the purpose.

   Needs improvement   Satisfactory   Excellent

Delivery

8. The speaker made good eye contact with the audience.

   Needs improvement   Satisfactory   Excellent

9. The volume of presentation was adequate.

   Needs improvement   Satisfactory   Excellent

10. The speaker's words were clear and could be understood.

    Needs improvement   Satisfactory   Excellent

The best part of this presentation was:

_____

_____

_____

A suggestion for improvement is:

_____

_____

_____

Name: _____ Date: _____

Evaluation Form: Standards of Reasoning

Activity

Speaker: _____ **Assignment:** _____

Directions: For 1–7, circle the choice that best describes the argument in the presentation. Then complete the sentence.

1. The reasons given were plentiful and varied enough to make the argument convincing.

   Needs improvement   Satisfactory   Excellent

2. The supporting evidence was factual and correct.

   Needs improvement   Satisfactory   Excellent

3. The reasons were clear and explained thoroughly.

   Needs improvement   Satisfactory   Excellent

4. The reasons and evidence were specific.

   Needs improvement   Satisfactory   Excellent

5. The reasons were strong and relevant to the issue.

   Needs improvement   Satisfactory   Excellent

6. The argument was logical, presented in sentences that seemed to go together in a sequence that made sense.

   Needs improvement   Satisfactory   Excellent

7. The explanation of the issue was fair.

   Needs improvement   Satisfactory   Excellent

The strongest part of the argument was:

_____

_____

_____

Name: _____ Date: _____

Prepare Questions for a Panel Discussion

Activity
21A

Directions: Use this chart to help you prepare questions for a panel discussion about issues of the 1940s and their evolution in the years that followed. In the left column, list the issues on which the panel discussion will focus. In the right column, list questions to related to each issue. Remember to write open-ended questions and to focus them on the purpose of the discussion.

Issue	Questions

Issue	Questions

Name: _____ Date: _____

Hamburger Model: Preserving History, Changing Society

Activity

Directions: Use the Hamburger Model to plan a persuasive essay explaining and defending your position on the relationship between efforts to preserve history and changes in society. Draft your essay on a separate sheet of paper.

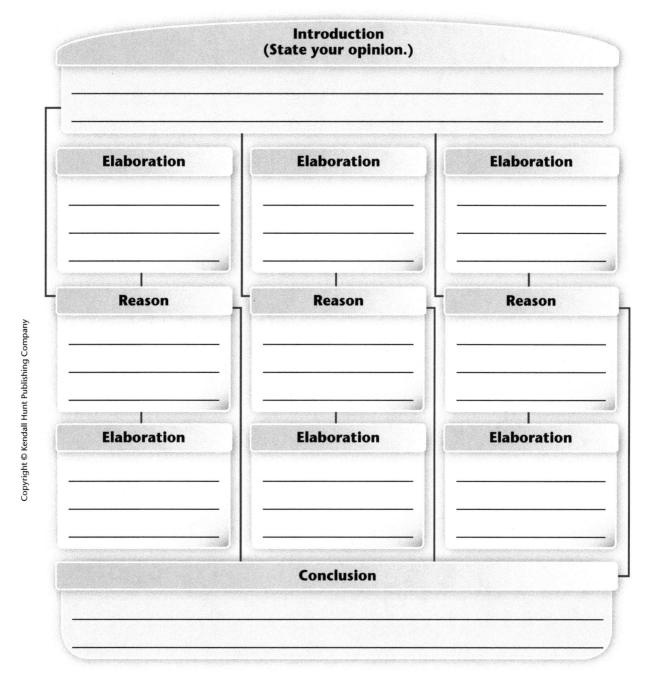

Introduction
(State your opinion.)

_____
_____

Elaboration

_____
_____
_____

Elaboration

_____
_____
_____

Elaboration

_____
_____
_____

Reason

_____
_____
_____

Reason

_____
_____
_____

Reason

_____
_____
_____

Elaboration

_____
_____
_____

Elaboration

_____
_____
_____

Elaboration

_____
_____
_____

Conclusion

_____
_____

Name: _____ Date: _____

Notes from a Panel Discussion

Directions: Use this chart to take notes on a panel discussion about issues of the 1940s and their evolution in the years that followed. In the left column, list the issues on which the panel discussion focuses. In the right column, note the most important ideas from the discussion.

Issue	Important Ideas

Issue	Important Ideas

Name: _____ Date: _____

Activity
22B

Self-Review of Writing

Assignment: _____

Directions: Review your writing carefully. For each sentence, circle the choice that best describes your writing. Then complete the two sentences.

1. My main idea is clear.

   Needs improvement   Satisfactory   Excellent

2. My details support the main idea.

   Needs improvement   Satisfactory   Excellent

3. My ideas flow smoothly and in an orderly way.

   Needs improvement   Satisfactory   Excellent

4. The structure clearly follows the Hamburger Model (introduction, body, conclusion).

   Needs improvement   Satisfactory   Excellent

5. My vocabulary is rich and varied.

   Needs improvement   Satisfactory   Excellent

My writing is strong in these ways:

_____

_____

_____

My writing could be improved in these ways:

_____

_____

_____

Name: _____ Date: _____

 **Activity**

Peer Review of Writing

Writer: _____ **Assignment:** _____

Directions: Read your partner's writing carefully. For each sentence, circle the choice that best describes the writing. Then complete the two sentences.

1. The main idea is clear.

   Needs improvement   Satisfactory   Excellent

2. The details support the main idea.

   Needs improvement   Satisfactory   Excellent

3. The ideas flow smoothly and in an orderly way.

   Needs improvement   Satisfactory   Excellent

4. The structure clearly follows the Hamburger Model (introduction, body, conclusion).

   Needs improvement   Satisfactory   Excellent

5. The vocabulary is rich and varied.

   Needs improvement   Satisfactory   Excellent

The writing is strong in these ways:

_____

_____

_____

The writing could be improved in these ways:

_____

_____

_____

Name: _____ Date: _____

Standards of Reasoning: Review of Writing

Activity

Directions: Evaluate the argument in "Address Unknown" by responding to the questions. Give examples to support your responses.

1. **Clarity:** Would anyone who reads the selection be able to understand its argument? Are the reasons clear? Are they explained thoroughly, or is more information needed?

_____

_____

_____

2. **Accuracy:** Is the supporting evidence factual and correct?

_____

_____

_____

3. **Precision:** Are the reasons and evidence specific, or are they general and vague?

_____

_____

_____

4. **Relevance:** How are the reasons and evidence connected to the question? Is the information important to the issue?

_____

_____

_____

Adapted from Paul, R. (1992). *Critical thinking: What every person needs to know to survive in a rapidly changing world.* Sonoma, CA: Foundation for Critical Thinking.

5. **Depth:** How does the writer address the complexities raised by the question? Are the arguments and reasons strong and important, or do they seem superficial?

_____

_____

_____

6. **Breadth:** Are enough different reasons given to make the argument convincing? Are different points of view presented? Is there another way to look at this question?

_____

_____

_____

7. **Logic:** Is the argument logical? Do the sentences seem to go together, and does their sequence make sense? Or does the selection sound like a set of disconnected statements?

_____

_____

_____

Name: _____ Date: _____

Activity

Change Model

Directions: List three examples that illustrate each of the generalizations about change.

Change

Change is linked to time.

_____
_____
_____

Change is everywhere.

_____
_____
_____

Change may be positive or negative.

_____
_____
_____

Change may be perceived as orderly or random.

_____
_____
_____

Change may happen naturally or may be caused by people.

_____
_____
_____

Name: _____ Date: _____

A Changing World:
Key Issues and Events

Activity

Directions: In the first row of the chart, list important social, political, and economic forces of the 1940s. In the second row, list how these forces have changed over the years from that decade to the present. In the final row, list predictions about how these forces will change in the future.

	Social Forces	**Political Forces**	**Economic Forces**
In the Past (1940s)			
To the Present (2010s)			
Into the Future (2060s)			

Name: _____ Date: _____

 **Activity**

23B

Final Writing Assignment

Directions: Think about how the literature, works of art and music, and historical events you have studied in this unit reflect the five generalizations about change. Select one generalization that seems especially true to you based on your studies. Write a persuasive essay arguing that this generalization is true, using a variety of specific examples from the unit readings and/or music, art, and historical events of the 1940s. Explain your reasons thoroughly, and write a conclusion to end your essay.

Name: _____ Date: _____

Hamburger Model: Final Writing Assignment

 **Activity**

Directions: Use the Hamburger Model to plan your final writing assignment.

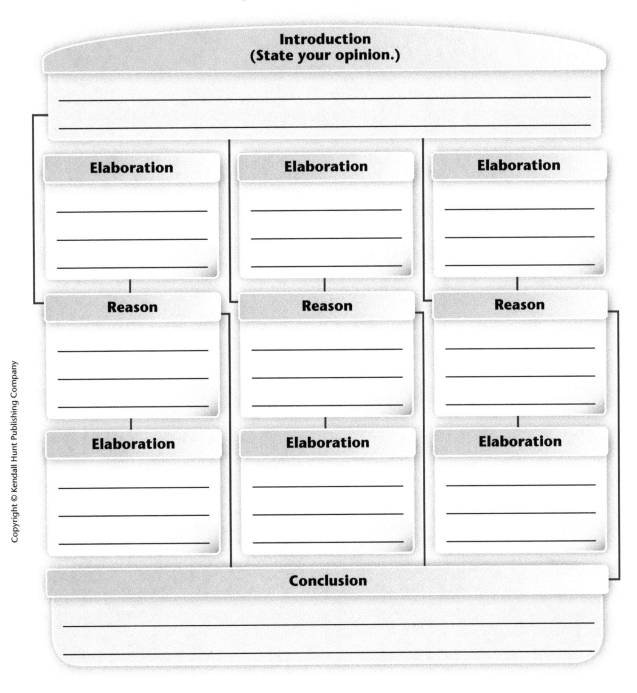

A Rose For Emily

William Faulkner

When Miss Emily Grierson died, our whole town went to her funeral: the men through a sort of respectful affection for a fallen monument, the women mostly out of curiosity to see the inside of her house, which no one save an old man-servant—a combined gardener and cook—had seen in at least ten years.

It was a big, squarish frame house that had once been white, decorated with cupolas and spires and scrolled balconies in the heavily lightsome style of the Seventies, set on what had once been our most select street. But garages and cotton gins had encroached and obliterated even the august names of that neighborhood; only Miss Emily's house was left, lifting its stubborn and coquettish decay above the cotton wagons and the gasoline pumps—an eyesore among eyesores. And now Miss Emily had gone to join the representatives of those august names where they lay in the cedar-bemused cemetery among the ranked and anonymous graves of Union and Confederate soldiers who fell at the battle of Jefferson.

Alive, Miss Emily had been a tradition, a duty, and a care; a sort of hereditary obligation upon the town, dating from that day in 1894 when Colonel Sartoris, the mayor—he who fathered the edict that no Negro woman should appear on the streets without an apron—remitted her taxes, the dispensation dating from the death of her father on into perpetuity. Not that Miss Emily would have accepted charity.

Colonel Sartoris invented an involved tale to the effect that Miss Emily's father had loaned money to the town, which the town, as a matter of business, preferred this way of repaying. Only a man of Colonel Sartoris' generation and thought could have invented it, and only a woman could have believed it.

When the next generation, with its more modern ideas, became mayors and aldermen, this arrangement created some little dissatisfaction. On the first of the year they mailed her a tax notice. February came, and there was no reply. They wrote her a formal letter, asking her to call at the sheriff's office at her convenience. A week later the mayor wrote her himself, offering to call or to send his car for her, and received in reply a note on paper of an archaic shape, in a thin, flowing calligraphy in faded ink, to the effect that she no longer went out at all. The tax notice was also enclosed, without comment.

They called a special meeting of the Board of Aldermen. A deputation waited upon her, knocked at the door through which no visitor had passed since she

Copyright © Kendall Hunt Publishing Company

ceased giving china-painting lessons eight or ten years earlier. They were admitted by the old Negro into a dim hall from which a stairway mounted into still more shadow. It smelled of dust and disuse—a close, dank smell. The Negro led them into the parlor. It was furnished in heavy, leather-covered furniture. When the Negro opened the blinds of one window, they could see that the leather was cracked; and when they sat down, a faint dust rose sluggishly about their thighs, spinning with slow motes in the single sun-ray. On a tarnished gilt easel before the fireplace stood a crayon portrait of Miss Emily's father.

They rose when she entered—a small, fat woman in black, with a thin gold chain descending to her waist and vanishing into her belt, leaning on an ebony cane with a tarnished gold head. Her skeleton was small and spare; perhaps that was why what would have been merely plumpness in another was obesity in her. She looked bloated, like a body long submerged in motionless water, and of that pallid hue. Her eyes, lost in the fatty ridges of her face, looked like two small pieces of coal pressed into a lump of dough as they moved from one face to another while the visitors stated their errand.

She did not ask them to sit. She just stood in the door and listened quietly until the spokesman came to a stumbling halt. Then they could hear the invisible watch ticking at the end of the gold chain.

Her voice was dry and cold. "I have no taxes in Jefferson. Colonel Sartoris explained it to me. Perhaps one of you can gain access to the city records and satisfy yourselves."

"But we have. We are the city authorities, Miss Emily. Didn't you get a notice from the sheriff, signed by him?"

"I received a paper, yes," Miss Emily said. "Perhaps he considers himself the sheriff ... I have no taxes in Jefferson."

"But there is nothing on the books to show that, you see. We must go by the—"

"See Colonel Sartoris. I have no taxes in Jefferson."

"But, Miss Emily—"

"See Colonel Sartoris." (Colonel Sartoris has been dead almost ten years.) "I have no taxes in Jefferson. Tobe!" The Negro appeared. "Show these gentlemen out."

. . .

So she vanquished them, horse and foot, just as she had vanquished their fathers thirty years before about the smell. That was two years after her father's death and a short time after her sweetheart—the one we believed would marry her—had deserted her. After her father's death she went out very little; after her sweetheart went away, people hardly saw her at all. A few of the ladies had the temerity to call, but were not received, and the only sign of life about the place was the Negro man—a young man then—going in and out with a market basket.

"Just as if a man—any man—could keep a kitchen properly," the ladies said; so they were not surprised when the smell developed. It was another link between the gross, teeming world and the high and mighty Griersons.

A neighbor, a woman, complained to the mayor, Judge Stevens, eighty years old.

"But what will you have me do about it, madam?" he said.

"Why, send her word to stop it," the woman said. "Isn't there a law?"

"I'm sure that won't be necessary," Judge Stevens said. "It's probably just a snake or a rat that nigger of hers killed in the yard. I'll speak to him about it."

The next day he received two more complaints, one from a man who came in diffident deprecation. "We really must do something about it, Judge. I'd be the last one in the world to bother Miss Emily, but we've got to do something." That night the Board of Aldermen met—three graybeards and one younger man, a member of the rising generation.

"It's simple enough," he said. "Send her word to have her place cleaned up. Give her a certain time to do it in, and if she don't …"

"Dammit, sir," Judge Stevens said, "will you accuse a lady to her face of smelling bad?"

So the next night, after midnight, four men crossed Miss Emily's lawn and slunk about the house like burglars, sniffing along the base of the brickwork and at the cellar openings while one of them performed a regular sowing motion with his hand out of a sack slung from his shoulder. They broke open the cellar door and sprinkled lime there, and in all the outbuildings. As they recrossed the lawn, a window that had been dark was lighted and Miss Emily sat in it, the light behind her, and her upright torso motionless as that of an idol. They crept quietly across the lawn and into the shadow of the locusts that lined the street. After a week or two the smell went away.

That was when people had begun to feel really sorry for her. People in our town, remembering how Old Lady Wyatt, her great-aunt, had gone completely crazy at last, believed that the Griersons held themselves a little too high for what they really were. None of the young men was quite good enough to Miss Emily and such. We had long thought of them as a tableau: Miss Emily a slender figure in white in the background, her father a spraddled silhouette in the foreground, his back to her and clutching a horsewhip, the two of them framed by the back-flung front door. So when she got to be thirty and was still single, we were not pleased exactly, but vindicated; even with insanity in the family she wouldn't have turned down all of her chances if they had really materialized.

When her father died, it got about that the house was all that was left to her; and in a way, people were glad. At last they could pity Miss Emily. Being left alone, and a pauper, she had become humanized. Now she too would know the old thrill and the old despair of a penny more or less.

The day after his death all the ladies prepared to call at the house and offer condolence and aid, as is our custom. Miss Emily met them at the door, dressed as usual and with no trace of grief on her face. She told them that her father was not dead. She did that for three days, with the ministers calling on her, and the doctors, trying to persuade her to let them dispose of the body. Just as they were about to resort to law and force, she broke down, and they buried her father quickly.

We did not say she was crazy then. We believed she had to do that. We remembered all the young men her father had driven away, and we knew that with nothing left, she would have to cling to that which had robbed her, as people will.

•   •   •

She was sick for a long time. When we saw her again, her hair was cut short, making her look like a girl, with a vague resemblance to those angels in colored church windows—sort of tragic and serene.

The town had just let the contracts for paving the sidewalks, and in the summer after her father's death they began the work. The construction company came with niggers and mules and machinery, and a foreman named Homer Barron, a Yankee—a big, dark, ready man, with a big voice and eyes lighter than his face. The little boys would follow in groups to hear him cuss the niggers, and the niggers singing in time to the rise and fall of picks. Pretty soon he knew everybody in town. Whenever you heard a lot of laughing anywhere about the square, Homer Barron would be in the center of the group. Presently we began to see him and Miss Emily on Sunday afternoons driving in the yellow-wheeled buggy and the matched team of bays from the livery stable.

At first we were glad that Miss Emily would have an interest, because the ladies all said, "Of course a Grierson would not think seriously of a Northerner, a day laborer." But there were still others, older people, who said that even grief could not cause a real lady to forget *noblesse oblige*—without calling it *noblesse oblige*. They just said, "Poor Emily. Her kinsfolk should come to her." She had some kin in Alabama; but years ago her father had fallen out with them over the estate of Old Lady Wyatt, the crazy woman, and there was no communication between the two families. They had not even been represented at the funeral.

And as soon as the old people said, "Poor Emily," the whispering began. "Do you suppose it's really so?" they said to one another. "Of course it is. What else could …" This behind their hands; rustling of craned silk and satin behind jalousies closed upon the sun of Sunday afternoon as the thin, swift clop-clop-clop of the matched team passed: "Poor Emily."

She carried her head high enough— even when we believed that she was fallen. It was as if she demanded more than ever the recognition of her dignity as the last Grierson; as if it had wanted that touch of earthiness to reaffirm her imperviousness. Like when she bought the rat poison, the arsenic. That was over a year after they had begun to say "Poor Emily," and while the two female cousins were visiting her.

"I want some poison," she said to the druggist. She was over thirty then, still a slight woman, though thinner than usual, with cold, haughty black eyes in a face the flesh of which was strained across the temples and about the eye-sockets as you imagine a lighthouse-keeper's face ought to look. "I want some poison," she said.

"Yes, Miss Emily. What kind? For rats and such? I'd recom—"

"I want the best you have. I don't care what kind."

The druggist named several. "They'll kill anything up to an elephant. But what you want is—"

"Arsenic," Miss Emily said. "Is that a good one?"

"Is … arsenic? Yes, ma'am. But what you want—"

"I want arsenic."

The druggist looked down at her. She looked back at him, erect, her face like a strained flag. "Why, of course," the druggist said. "If that's what you want. But the law requires you to tell what you are going to use it for."

Miss Emily just stared at him, her head tilted back in order to look him eye for eye, until he looked away and went and got the arsenic and wrapped it up. The Negro delivery boy brought her the package; the druggist didn't come back. When she opened the package at home there was written on the box, under the skull and bones: "For rats."

So the next day we all said, "She will kill herself'; and we said it would be the best thing. When she had first begun to be seen with Homer Barron, we had said, "She will marry him." Then we said, "She will persuade him yet," because Homer himself had remarked—he liked men, and it was known that he drank with the younger men in the Elks' Club—that he was not a marrying man. Later we said, "Poor Emily" behind the jalousies as they passed on Sunday afternoon in the glittering buggy, Miss Emily with her

Copyright © Kendall Hunt Publishing Company

head high and Homer Barron with his hat cocked and a cigar in his teeth, reins and whip in a yellow glove.

Then some of the ladies began to say that it was a disgrace to the town and a bad example to the young people. The men did not want to interfere, but at last the ladies forced the Baptist minister— Miss Emily's people were Episcopal—to call upon her. He would never divulge what happened during that interview, but he refused to go back again. The next Sunday they again drove about the streets, and the following day the minister's wife wrote to Miss Emily's relations in Alabama.

So she had blood-kin under her roof again and we sat back to watch developments. At first nothing happened. Then we were sure that they were to be married. We learned that Miss Emily had been to the jeweler's and ordered a man's toilet set in silver, with the letters H. B. on each piece. Two days later we learned that she had bought a complete outfit of men's clothing, including a nightshirt, and we said, "They are married." We were really glad. We were glad because the two female cousins were even more Grierson than Miss Emily had ever been.

So we were not surprised when Homer Barron—the streets had been finished some time since—was gone. We were a little disappointed that there was not a public blowing-off, but we believed that he had gone on to prepare for Miss Emily's coming, or to give her a chance to get rid of the cousins. (By that time it was a cabal, and we were all Miss Emily's allies to help circumvent the cousins.) Sure enough, after another week they departed. And, as we had expected all along, within three days Homer Barron was back in town. A neighbor saw the Negro man admit him at the kitchen door at dusk one evening.

And that was the last we saw of Homer Barron. And of Miss Emily for some time. The Negro man went in and out with the market basket, but the front door remained closed. Now and then we would see her at a window for a moment, as the men did that night when they sprinkled the lime, but for almost six months she did not appear on the streets. Then we knew that this was to be expected too; as if that quality of her father which had thwarted her woman's life so many times had been too virulent and too furious to die.

When we next saw Miss Emily, she had grown fat and her hair was turning gray. During the next few years it grew grayer and grayer until it attained an even pepper-and-salt iron-gray, when it ceased turning. Up to the day of her death at seventy-four it was still that vigorous iron-gray, like the hair of an active man.

From that time on her front door remained closed, save for a period of six or seven years, when she was about forty, during which she gave lessons in china-painting. She fitted up a studio in one of the downstairs rooms, where the daughters and granddaughters of Colonel Sartoris' contemporaries were sent to her with the same regularity and in the same spirit that they were sent to church on Sundays with a twenty-five-cent piece for the collection plate. Meanwhile her taxes had been remitted.

Then the newer generation became the backbone and the spirit of the town, and the painting pupils grew up and fell away and did not send their children to her with boxes of color and tedious brushes and pictures cut from the ladies' magazines. The front door closed upon the last one and remained closed for good. When the town got free postal delivery, Miss Emily alone refused to let them fasten the metal numbers above her door and attach a mailbox to it. She would not listen to them.

Daily, monthly, yearly we watched the Negro grow grayer and more stooped, going in and out with the market basket. Each December we sent her a tax notice, which would be returned by the post office a week later; unclaimed. Now and then we would see her in one of the downstairs windows—she had evidently shut up the top floor of the house—like the carven torso of an idol in a niche, looking or not looking at us, we could never tell which. Thus she passed from generation to generation—dear, inescapable, impervious, tranquil, and perverse.

And so she died. Fell ill in the house filled with dust and shadows, with only a doddering Negro man to wait on her. We did not even know she was sick; we had long since given up trying to get any information from the Negro. He talked to no one, probably not even to her, for his voice had grown harsh and rusty, as if from disuse.

She died in one of the downstairs rooms, in a heavy walnut bed with a curtain, her gray head propped on a pillow yellow and moldy with age and lack of sunlight.

·   ·   ·

The Negro met the first of the ladies at the front door and let them in, with their hushed, sibilant voices and their quick, curious glances, and then he disappeared. He walked right through the house and out the back and was not seen again.

The two female cousins came at once. They held the funeral on the second day, with the town coming to look at Miss Emily beneath a mass of bought flowers, with the crayon face of her father musing profoundly above the bier and the ladies sibilant and macabre; and the very old men—some in their brushed Confederate uniforms—on the porch and the lawn, talking of Miss Emily as if she had been a contemporary of theirs, believing that they had danced with her and courted her perhaps, confusing time with its mathematical progression, as the old do, to whom all the past is not a diminishing road but, instead, a huge meadow which no winter ever quite touches, divided from them now by the narrow bottle-neck of the most recent decade of years.

Already we knew that there was one room in that region above stairs which no one had seen in forty years, and which would have to be forced. They waited until Miss Emily was decently in the ground before they opened it.

The violence of breaking down the door seemed to fill this room with pervading dust. A thin, acrid pall as of the tomb seemed to lie everywhere upon this room decked and furnished as for a bridal: upon the valance curtains of faded rose color, upon the rose-shaded lights, upon the dressing table, upon the delicate array of crystal and the man's toilet things backed with tarnished silver, silver so tarnished that the monogram was obscured. Among them lay a collar and tie, as if they had just been removed, which, lifted, left upon the surface a pale crescent in the dust. Upon a chair hung the suit, carefully folded; beneath it the two mute shoes and the discarded socks.

The man himself lay in the bed.

For a long while we just stood there, looking down at the profound and fleshless grin. The body had apparently once lain in the attitude of an embrace, but now the long sleep that outlasts love, that conquers even the grimace of love, had cuckolded him. What was left of him, rotted beneath what was left of the nightshirt, had become inextricable from the bed in which he lay; and upon him and upon the pillow beside him lay that even coating of the patient and biding dust.

Then we noticed that in the second pillow was the indentation of a head. One of us lifted something from it, and leaning forward, that faint and invisible dust dry and acrid in the nostrils, we saw a long strand of iron-gray hair.

Inspecting Our Own Ideas: Student Grammar Study

by Michael C. Thompson

As you begin to read this short study of grammar and to think about the ideas you will find here, you should know that there is one important purpose for what you are doing. It is not to learn a large number of facts, or to memorize terms, or to score points. Lots of grammar books can help you learn facts and terms. This study is different. Its purpose is to show you the deeper meaning of grammar that is usually missing from the grammar fact books—the part that many people never understand.

What is this deeper meaning?

It is that grammar is a kind of magic lens, a secret thinking method we can use to peek inside our own minds and to detect the designs of our own ideas.

Using grammar this way, we can learn about ourselves, learn about what makes us human, learn about why some ideas are clear and others are confused, learn about beautiful ways to share our thoughts with other people.

In order to make the most of what you will read, you should understand from the beginning that even though there will be facts and details to learn, the facts are not the point. The point is the point. And so as you read, do what the coaches always tell you: keep your eye on the ball.

Do not forget that you are concentrating on the deep thinking, the deep meaning, the ability to appreciate the real power of grammar.

The best way to do this is to begin by previewing the study with your teacher. Look over it together, and agree on how much you should read in your first session. Then go read, and think, and reread. Make notes on your ideas and on the questions you have that the reading doesn't answer. Then meet with your teacher to talk about what you have learned and to look over any of the written exercises you may have done. Keep working in this way until you have read the entire grammar study and can discuss it completely with your teacher or other students, depending upon your class situation.

Remember that grammar is a kind of higher order thinking, like logic or mathematics. Grammar can show us secrets that no other thinking method can show us. If you read and think carefully, you will never forget that grammar is a wonderful tool for the mind.

1. Ideas, Language, and Grammar

How do we talk to each other?

How do we write to each other?

How do we read what someone else has written?

We use **language**. Language is our way of putting words together to make our **ideas**.

Any time we use words to **say something about something**, that is an idea!

We have to **say something ... about something**.

In other words, an idea is made of **two parts**. One part is **what we are talking about**, and the other part is **what we are saying about it**.

We might say something about ourselves. Or we might say something about an object, such as a distant spiral galaxy in deep space, or a glowing hologram, or a thundering Triceratops. We might say something about wizened old wizard's grizzled countence. If we did that, we might say. "The wizened old wizard's grizzled countenance grinned out at us from under his hat."

Do you see the two parts of that idea?

What we are talking about:

 The wizened old wizard's grizzled countenance

What we are saying about it:

 grinned out at us from under his hat.

In this idea, we are using words in language to make an idea about a wizard's countenance.

Of course, it helps to know that *wizened* means wrinkled and withered, that *grizzled* means gray, and that a *countenance* is a person's personality as seen in his or her face. In other words, a wizened old wizard's grizzled countenance is a wrinkled, gray-haired wizard's face. We see such a wizard, named Gandalf, in J.R.R. Tolkien's famous books, *The Hobbit* and the *Lord of the Rings* series.

But back to language and ideas. Another idea could be, "This is my letter to the world." In this idea, we are saying something about something. Part one: we are talking about *this*. Part two: what are we saying about *this*? That it is our letter to the world. Of course, this idea comes from a very famous poem by Emily Dickinson, one of America's very greatest poets. And when she said "This is my letter to the world," she was referring to her own poem. But Emily Dickinson never achieved fame during her lifetime, and she led a lonely life. Her poem continues: "This is my letter to the world / That never wrote to me."

So, ideas have two parts.

But guess what? We have a very special way to study ideas that we make out of words in language. This special way to study language is called **grammar**. That's right, grammar. You have studied grammar before, I know, but did you ever think of grammar as a way of thinking?

Grammar is a way of thinking about language.

Using grammar, we can inspect one of our own language ideas, and see how it is made! We can do important things with grammar. We can find an idea's two parts, and we can find all of the groups of words in the idea, and we can even look at each word by itself and see what it does to make the idea work. We can study the invisible architecture of ideas. This helps us to understand ourselves, and to understand how we think! In the pages that follow, you will learn some advanced ideas about grammar, and about how grammar helps us to understand our own ideas.

Review

Let's look again at the ideas we have discussed. Think carefully about each of these points:

language: our way of putting words together to express our ideas

idea: a two-part thought about something

the two parts of an idea: what we are talking about, and what we are saying about it

grammar: a special way of thinking about language

2. Sentences: Subject and Predicate

In grammar, we have a special word to describe an idea that is made of two parts. This special word is *sentence*. A sentence is an idea. We sometimes say that a sentence is a **complete thought**, but this is just a different way of saying the same thing—that a sentence is an idea.

You have undoubtedly studied the sentence before, but in this discussion we are going to examine the sentence in some new ways that you may never have considered. You will see that the sentence is far more important than you may have realized.

You may not know that our English word *sentence* comes from a very old word, *sententia,* which was a Latin word used thousands of years ago by the ancient Romans. To the Romans, the word *sententia* meant "way of thinking." We will see that many of the words used in grammar have very logical meanings that are based on ancient Latin or Greek words.

Now, we learned that a sentence is an idea that is complete. But what makes a sentence's idea complete?

It is complete because it has both of the two parts that it needs to make sense to someone. Until it has both of these two important parts, it is not finished, not complete.

Let's think about this more deeply. If I wish to understand you, then there are two things that I need to know:

I need to know **what you are talking about**,

and

I need to know **what you are saying about it**.

If I do know these two things, then I can understand you. But if I do not know what you are talking about, or if I do not know what you are trying to say about it, then I will not understand you.

Grammar gives us names for these two parts of the sentence. The usual first part of the sentence, what it is about, is called the **subject**. The second part of the sentence, what we are saying about the subject, is called the **predicate**. Of course, there are times when the normal order of the sentence is disturbed, and the predicate comes before the subject, but we will not focus on that for the moment. Let's look at some examples of sentences:

Subject	**Predicate**
(What the idea is about)	(What we are saying about the subject)
Thoreau	went to the woods to live deliberately.
Tillie	is the stream I go a-fishin in.
Our life	is frittered away by detail.
This	is my letter to the world.
Nobody	ever helps me into carriages.
(You)	Look at my arm!
The woods	are lovely, dark and deep.
My little horse	gives his harness bells a shake.
Whoso	would be a man, must be a nonconformist.
It	is I, Hamlet the Dane.
I	am.

Notice that a sentence does not have to be long. Sometimes a sentence only has two words in it. "Pterodactyls landed" is a sentence. Even though it is short, it has a subject, *Pterodactyls*, and a predicate, *landed*.

(Do you know what **pterodactyls** were? They were flying dinosaurs that had wings of skin, and that became extinct at the end of the Mesozoic era. In Arizona fossil pterodactyls have been found that had 40-foot wingspans. They are called *pterodactyls* because they had clawed fingers in the middle of their wings, and so their scientific name comes from the ancient Greek *pter*, which means wing, and *dactyl*, which means finger. A second question: do you know what the **Mesozoic** era was? Well, *meso* means middle, and *zo* means animal. The Mesozoic era was a geologic era in the earth's history that occurred after the Paleozoic era and before the Cenozoic era, from 230,000,000 years ago until 65,000,000 years ago. The Mesozoic era featured the rise and fall of the dinosaurs, the appearance of birds, grasses, and flowering plants. Now, if you are really adventurous, you will go look up the Paleozoic era, and see what happened then!)

Notice that a subject or a predicate by itself is not an idea; it is only a **fragment**, or piece, of an idea. **A sentence fragment** is an incomplete piece of a sentence; it only makes an incomplete thought. A sentence fragment needs to be finished, just like the subjects and predicates above needed to be finished.

Now, why is all of this so important? Because by using grammar to examine the way we communicate in language, we have noticed something really amazing. In our speech and writing, we say millions of things in millions of ways, and you would expect that in all of this multitudinous expression, there would be a very large number of basic forms to use for expressing our ideas. But this is not the case. At the core of our millions of expressions, there is an astonishing simplicity: the subject/predicate pair. When we exclaim, or make earnest declarations, or ask questions, or tell jokes, or profess our love, or express our anger, or confess our sadness, we always use the same secret, magical formula: the subject/predicate pair.

This simple, two-part architecture is the hidden form that underpins every idea we utter.

If you spend two hours on the phone with your friend, and each of you utters 2,000 ideas to the other, all 4,000 of your ideas will have been expressed by means of the same silent structure, the subject/predicate pair.

Why?

Because human language has evolved to accommodate the needs of the human mind. And the mind needs the two-part structure. The simplicity. A–B. 1–2. Computers operate on what is called **binary code**, and communicate all of their programs by means of 1's or 0's, ones or zeros. The human mind is that way.

It wants to know, about all groups of words, WHAT ARE YOU TALKING ABOUT? WHAT ARE YOU SAYING ABOUT IT?

What is the subject?

What is the predicate?

Understanding this gives us great insight into all forms of clear communication, because this subject/predicate law must be applied not only to the sentence but to all levels of communication. **For your sentence**, what are you talking about, and what are you saying about it? **For your paragraph**, what are you talking about, and what are you saying about it? **For your essay**, what are you talking about, and what are you saying about it? **For any level of communication** whatsoever, what is your subject, and what is your predicate?

Now we can understand why English teachers spend so much time helping you to write clear sentences, helping you to write organized paragraphs with topic sentences, and helping you to write essays that have clear central ideas.

Concealed in the sentence, like a prehistoric insect trapped in amber, is a model of the mind. This model is a double question:

What is your subject?/What is your predicate?

Review

Now, let's look again at the new ideas we have learned about language and sentences.

Our way of putting words together to make our ideas is called **language**.

A two-part thought about something is called an **idea**.

What we are talking about and what we are saying about it are the **two parts of an idea**.

A special way of thinking about language is called **grammar**.

In grammar, we call a two-part idea a **sentence**.

The two parts of the sentence are called the subject and the **predicate**.

What the sentence is about is called the **subject**.

What we are saying about the subject is called the **predicate**.

A piece of a sentence that is not complete is only a **fragment**.

A sentence is a **model of the mind**.

A Vocabulary Note: The word **subject** contains two ancient Latin word pieces, or stems, that we see in many words, **sub**, and **ject**. The stem **sub** means "under," and we see **sub** in words such as **submarine** and **submerge**. The stem **ject** means "throw," and we see **ject** in words such as **eject** and **dejected**. So the word **subject** actually contains a picture: the **subject** of a sentence is the part that is "thrown down" for discussion. Look up some of the following example words in your dictionary, carefully study their etymologies, and see if you can understand *why* they mean what they mean:

Stem	Meaning	Example Words
sub	under	submarine, submerge, subdue, subtract, subside, subordinate
ject	throw	reject, dejected, interject, eject, conjecture, project, adjective

3. Clauses: The Sentences Within Sentences

There is another surprising fact about the way we make our ideas into sentences. Many of the sentences that we use are just like the ones we studied above. They have a subject, and then a predicate, and then the sentence ends. But sometimes our ideas get so connected that we like to join simple ideas together into a longer, more complicated idea. In other words, sometimes, we join related sentences together into a longer, more complicated sentence. For example,

We might have these two sentences:

Congress passed the bill. The president signed it into law.

Each of these sentences has its own subject and predicate. But since these two sentences describe something that happened in a connected event, we can connect the sentences together into a longer sentence:

Congress passed the bill, and the president signed it into law.

Now the two short sentences make one long sentence, and it has one subject and predicate, followed by a second subject and predicate, all in one sentence!

Congress	**passed the bill,**	and	**the president**	**signed it into law.**
subject	predicate		subject	predicate

When we join short sentences this way into a longer sentence of subject/predicate chains, we call each little subject/predicate group a **clause**.

Congress passed the bill,	and	**the president signed it into law.**
first clause		second clause

When there is only one subject/predicate set in the sentence, we say that the sentence has **one clause**.

Our word *clause* comes from the ancient Latin word *claudere* which meant "to close" to the Romans. This makes sense even now, because a clause is a group of words in which an idea gets opened, and closed. The idea is opened when we introduce a subject, and then it is closed when we provide the predicate. In a long sentence made of many clauses, we open and close a number of related ideas in a row. Let's look at some examples of clauses in sentences. Notice that each clause has its own subject and its own predicate:

Clauses in Sentences

1. <u>Our forefathers</u>   <u>brought forth upon this continent a new nation.</u>
        subject   predicate

a one-clause sentence

2. <u>I</u>   <u>will arise,</u>   and   <u>I</u>   <u>will go now.</u>
  subj.   predicate   subj.   predicate

     first clause   second clause

a two-clause sentence

3. <u>Robert Frost</u>   <u>has miles to go</u>   before   <u>he</u>   <u>sleeps.</u>
     subject   predicate   subj.   predicate

     first clause   second clause

a two-clause sentence

4. When   <u>the attack</u>   <u>finally begins,</u>   <u>you</u>   <u>sneak up quietly,</u>   and
          subject   predicate   subj.   predicate

     first clause   second clause

<u>the gang</u>   <u>will throw balloons.</u>
  subject   predicate

     third clause

a three-clause sentence

See? We can make long sentences out of any number of related ideas!

But why is it important to know this?

By using grammar to inspect our own ideas, we have discovered that our brains can understand ideas and the relationships between different ideas so well and so quickly that we can connect these ideas into sentences of related clauses faster than we can even speak. We can do it without even knowing we are doing it, and before we even have a name for it. It is only now, when we use grammar to inspect our ideas, that we begin to realize what powerful things our minds are. The grammar of clauses shows us how our minds build beautiful structures of ideas.

Of course, not all clauses are the same. They are all alike because they all have their own subjects and predicates, but some clauses make sense all by themselves, whereas other clauses only make sense if they are connected to other clauses. For example, in the sentence "As Michelangelo painted the fresco on the Sistine Chapel ceiling, the paint dripped into his eyes," there are two clauses. The first clause is "As Michelangelo painted the fresco on the Sistine Chapel ceiling," and the second clause is "the paint dripped into his eyes." Notice that each clause has its own subject and predicate. But also notice that the two clauses are different. The second clause in the sentence would make sense as a sentence by itself:

The paint dripped into his eyes.

The first clause, by itself, is not a complete idea:

As Michelangelo painted the fresco on the Sistine Chapel ceiling.

The Sistine Chapel ceiling, by the way, is one of the great works of art of all time. The Sistine Chapel is the principal chapel in the Vatican in Rome. It was built by Pope Sixtus IV, and it contains Michelangelo's (1475–1564) famous fresco of scenes from the Bible, which Michelangelo painted upside down from scaffolding. You will appreciate how difficult this was when you realize that fresco paintings are painted on wet plaster, and have to be completed before the plaster dries; Michelangelo had to apply wet plaster to the ceiling as he lay face up on a scaffold high above the floor, and then paint quickly so the paint would soak in. Only much later could he get down from the scaffolding and look up to see how his work looked from a distance. Time, bad restorations, and pollution have damaged the fresco, and a 1980s restoration which made the colors of the ceiling much brighter and more vivid than they have been for years has been very controversial because many people preferred the aged look of browns and gray tones which the painting had acquired over the years. The story of Michelangelo's ordeal in painting the ceiling is one of the most interesting stories in history, and you would really enjoy reading about it.

But back to clauses. As usual, grammar assigns logical names to these two kinds of clauses. Clauses which are independent, and can stand alone as sentences by themselves, are called **independent clauses**, and clauses which depend on being connected to other clauses in order to have their ideas completed are called **dependent clauses**.

Based on the number and type of clauses a sentence contains, it is classified into a type of **sentence structure. A simple sentence** is a simple one that only has one independent clause. A **compound sentence** is compounded of two or more independent clauses. And a **complex sentence** is a complex one that has both an independent clause and a dependent clause, in either order.

Here are some examples of clauses from Henry David Thoreau's writings:

Simple: This world is a place of business.

Compound: Things do not change; we change.

Complex: I went to the woods because I wished to live deliberately.

Here are some examples from a speech by Sojourner Truth:

Simple: Look at my arm!

Compound: Nobody ever helps me into carriages or over puddles, and ain't I a woman?

Complex: When I cried out with my mother's grief, none but Jesus heard me.

Are you beginning to appreciate how fast and wonderful your brain is, that it can handle these complicated forms of ideas so effortlessly?

We have looked at sentence **structures**, but sentences also have purposes. Once again, these are so well named that they almost define themselves. **Declarative sentences** declare things; in other words, they make statements. "I love the ocean" is a declarative sentence. **Imperative sentences** are imperious, like emperors; they give commands. "Bring me an ocean" is an imperative sentence, though a foolish one. Notice that in an imperative sentence, the subject is not expressed, but is only understood: (You) bring me an ocean. **Interrogative sentences** interrogate; they ask questions. "Where is the ocean?" is an interrogative sentence. And **exclamatory sentences** exclaim, or cry out. "Here comes the ocean!" is an exclamatory sentence.

Declarative sentences declare.

Imperative sentences are imperious.

Interrogative sentences interrogate.

Exclamatory sentences exclaim.

It's easy to remember the sentence purposes.

4. Parts of Speech: The Kinds of Words

No matter how many clauses a sentence contains, one thing you have noticed about all ideas or sentences: every sentence is made of words. There are many thousands of words in our language. In fact, there are far more words than anyone could ever learn!

Just imagine that you traveled to a land far, far away.

(One faraway land is Nepal, near Tibet in the continent of Asia, where Mount Everest, the highest mountain in the world, is. Mount Everest is 29,028 feet high, and it is in the Himalayan mountain range. It is so high that it has only been climbed a few times. Nepal's high-altitude capital is Katmandu. There is a wonderful novel you will want to read one day, *Lost Horizon*, written by James Hilton in 1933, that depicts Nepal under the fictitious name of "Shangri-La.")

Now, just imagine that you travel to a land far, far away, and the gray-bearded king of the land says, "You may have all of the treasures in my kingdom if you can tell me how many kinds of words there are." The king then looks down to the green valleys far, far below, and an icy wind comes down from the frozen peaks above, and blows through your hair.

What would you say? There are thousands and thousands of words in the dictionary. Are there thousands of kinds of words? Are there hundreds of kinds of words?

Well, you are in luck, because if you set off on an adventure one day, you will be prepared with the knowledge that there are only eight kinds of words! Just imagine! All of those words in the dictionary can be put into only eight piles, and the eight different kinds of words are easy to learn. We call the eight kinds of words the eight **parts of speech** because all of our speech can be *parted* into only eight piles of words.

The eight parts of speech are the *noun, pronoun, adjective, verb, adverb preposition, conjunction,* and *interjection.* Let's look at them closely:

The Parts of Speech

Part of Speech	Function	Examples
noun (n.)	name of something	*Mary, dog, garden, sound*

A noun is the name of a person, *Picasso*, or the name of a place, *Amsterdam*, or the name of a thing, *aurora*. The sentence *The wind in the willows whispered in the leaves* has three nouns: wind, willows, and leaves. Nouns give us names for things!

Nouns can be **singular**, like *dog*, or **plural**, like *dogs*. **Proper nouns**, like *Istanbul*, are capitalized, but **common nouns**, like *boot*, are not capitalized.

pronoun (pron.)	replaces a noun	*I, she, him, it, them*

A pronoun is a short word that replaces a usually longer noun so that we can speak faster. For example, instead of always saying a person's name such as *Abraham Lincoln* in a sentence, we can say *he*. In the sentence *"He was born in a log cabin in Illinois,"* the nouns *Abraham* and *Lincoln* have been replaced by the short pronoun *he*. Pronouns make language fast!

Two common kinds of pronouns are the **subject pronouns**:

I, you, he, she, it, we, you, they

and the **object pronouns**:

me, you, him, her, it, us, you, them.

These two kinds of pronouns are so important that you must have them **memorized**. (I'm serious!) You will see why later.

In discussing pronouns, we classify them according to person. Here is how the classification scheme works for the subject pronouns:

Copyright © Kendall Hunt Publishing Company

	Singular	Plural
First Person	**I**	**we**
Second Person	**you**	**you**
Third Person	**he, she, it**	**they**

Notice that the third person singular pronouns are also divided into the three genders: masculine, feminine, and neuter.

We have learned that every sentence has a subject and a predicate. And every subject contains either a noun or a pronoun. This noun or pronoun that the sentence is about is sometimes called the **simple subject**. The **complete subject** is the noun and all of the accompanying words.

adjective (adj.)

modifies a noun or pronoun　　　*red, tall, fast, good, the*

To modify is to *change*. An adjective is a word that changes the meaning of a noun or pronoun. For example, for the noun *tree*, we can change it by saying *tall* tree, or *Christmas* tree, or *cherry* tree, and each of these different adjectives changes (we sometimes say *modifies*) the noun and gives us a different picture in our minds. Another example: the noun *garden* could be modified by either the adjective *flower* or the adjective *secret*. We could talk about a *flower* garden, but we could use a different adjective and talk about a *secret* garden instead, and that would modify the idea. Some adjectives are the opposites of one another: a *fast* car is the opposite of a *slow* car.

The most common adjectives are the three little words *a*, *an*, and *the*. These three adjectives are called the **articles**. The word *the* is called the **definite article**, and the words *a* and *an* are called the **indefinite articles**.

Notice that the noun, pronoun, and adjective go together and work together. The nouns name things, the pronouns replace the nouns, and the adjectives modify either nouns or pronouns. You could say that the noun, with its supporting pronouns and adjectives, forms a little noun system, like the sun with its planets.

verb (v.)

an action or equals word　　*jumps, fell, is*

Every sentence contains a verb, which is sometimes called the **simple predicate**. The **complete predicate** is the verb and all of its accompanying words that say something about the subject.

There are two kinds of verbs:

Action verbs show action; they show people and things doing things. Look at the action verbs in these sentences: The dog *barked*. The tall man *grinned*. My best friend *reads* lots of books. We *drove* to Florida. Mary *opened* her brown eyes.

Linking verbs are equals words; they show that two things are the same. For example, in the sentence "Siegfried is a good student." the verb *is* means that Siegfried and the good student are the same person. Siegfried IS the good student.

Action: Michelangelo *ran* after the ball.

Linking: Michelangelo *is* good at soccer.

Action: Donatello *drew* a sketch.

Linking: Donatello *is* a genius.

Action: Raphael *plays* baseball in the spring.

Linking: Raphael *is* a pitcher on the baseball team.

My favorite linking verb sentence is by the poet Marianne Moore, who said that poems *are* imaginary gardens with real toads in them. Don't you like that idea?

Parts of the Sentence: We have learned about two parts of the sentence already, the **simple subject** and the **simple predicate**, or verb. Well, there are two other parts of the sentence you can identify if you know what kind of verb you have. When an action verb sentence shows the subject doing something to something, as in the sentence "The dog bit the mailman," we call the noun or pronoun that receives the action a **direct object**. But when a linking verb sentence shows that the subject is equal to something else, as in the sentence "The dog is a poodle," we call the noun or pronoun that is linked to the subject a **subject complement**.

Direct Object: Achilles grabbed the **warrior**.

Subject Complement: Achilles was a **warrior**.

Notice that the only way to tell whether the second noun in these sentences is a direct object or a subject complement is to look at the verb. If a sentence contains an action verb, it might have a direct object, but if the sentence contains a linking verb, it might have a subject complement. This is a very advanced grammar idea, and it gives us deep insight into the way we form our own ideas.

Verb Tense: Another very important fact: verbs change, according to the *time* they are describing. The basic form of the verb is called the **infinitive form**, because it is not limited or finite in time. The infinitive always begins with the word *to*, and we refer to verbs such as *to fly, to do, to go,* and so forth. The time-limited forms of the verb are called the verb tenses. The three most familiar verb tenses are the **present tense**, the **past tense**, and the **future tense**. The verb *to play,* for example, takes these forms:

Present tense: I *play* softball.

Past tense: I *played* softball.

Future tense: I *will play* softball.

There are also three other tenses, called the **perfect tenses**. These are named after the Latin word *perficere,* which means "finished." The perfect tenses show action that is finished by using a helping verb:

Present perfect tense: I *have played* softball.

Past perfect tense: I *had played* softball.

Future perfect tense: I *will have played* softball.

In addition to tense, verbs also have voice, either **active voice** or **passive voice**. Verbs can be voiced in a way that portrays the subject as active, or they can be voiced in a way that portrays the subject as passive. For example, the verb *to strike* can be voiced in these ways:

Active voice: The meteor *struck* the ship.

Passive voice: The ship was *struck* by the meteor.

Notice that in both sentences, the verb is *to strike,* and in both sentences the tense is past tense. The only difference is the voicing of the verb to indicate the active or passive nature of the subject.

adverb (adv.)

| **modifies a verb, adj., or adv.** | ***quickly, slowly, well*** |

An adverb is a word that modifies or changes the meaning of a verb, an adjective, or another adverb.

Adverb modifies verb: I swam *quickly.*

Adverb modifies adverb: I swam *very* quickly.

Adverb modifies adjective: I saw a *very* red star.

Before you continue reading, study these three examples very carefully, and make sure you understand every part of speech in these three sentence.

Notice that many adverbs end in *ly,* such as *quickly, slowly, loudly, nearly, badly,* and *hungrily.*

The verb and adverb form a little system together. Just as the noun is often accompanied by an adjective, the verb is often accompanied by an adverb that gives it new meaning.

Just as adjectives help us adjust the meanings of nouns when the nouns are not quite what we mean, adverbs help us adjust the meanings of verbs. Adjectives and adverbs are **modifiers** that help us adjust the meanings of nouns and verbs.

preposition (prep.)

shows relationship   *in, on, beside, after*

A preposition is a word that shows how two things are related to each other in space, direction, or time. Space examples: The dog was *on* the dock. The book is *in* the drawer. The boy was *inside* the secret garden. The garden was *behind* the wall. Direction examples: The money is *for* you. The boat moved *toward* the dock. Time examples: The movie is *after* the news. My birthday is *before* yours. She got sick *during* the game. Prepositions are little words, but they are very important because they show where everything is in space and time. They give language its physics. Prepositions let us make ideas that show how the world is arranged!

Another interesting fact about prepositions is that they are always found in word groups, such as **in** *the box,* **on** *the dock,* **under** *the bed,* **around** *the world,* and **over** *the rainbow.* These little word groups always begin with prepositions, and they are called **prepositional phrases**.

In fact, the word *preposition* is made of the Latin *pre,* which means *before,* and the word *position.* A preposition is called a preposition because its **position is always before** the other words in the prepositional phrase! It has the pre-position.

In a prepositional phrase such as *on the dock, over the rainbow, for her,* or *in the beginning,* we call the noun or pronoun that the preposition is relating to something the **object of preposition**.

We will study phrases more below, but now we can note that prepositional phrases serve as modifiers. A prepositional phrase will either act like an adjective, or it will act like an adverb. In the sentence, "The dog on the dock barked," the prepositional phrase *on the dock* acts as an adjective to modify the noun *dog*.

conjunction (conj.)

joins words   *and, or, but, so, yet*

A conjunction is a word that joins two other words together into a pair. Michael *and* David ate many hot dogs. By using the conjunction *and,* we can join the two nouns *Michael* and

David together, so we can talk about them both at once, as a pair. We can use a conjunction to join two pronouns: Give the lithograph to him *or* her. If we want to, we can even use a conjunction to join two verbs: Mary thought *and* wondered. We can use a conjunction to join two adverbs: He spoke quickly, *but* confidently. Or we can use a conjunction to join two adjectives: The wall was high *and* dark. Conjunctions let us join things into pairs!

Would you like one more very interesting example? You can even use a conjunction to join two **groups of words** together! For example, you can use a conjunction to join two prepositional phrases together: The albatross flew **over the ship** *and* **around the mast**.

There are different kinds of conjunctions. **Coordinating conjunctions** (the complete list of coordinating conjunctions is *and, but, or, nor, for, so,* and *yet*) are used to join things of equal value, such as the two names in a compound subject: "Brutus *and* Cassius plotted against Caesar." The **subordinating conjunctions** (such as *if, as, since, when, because*) are used to join things of unequal value, such as the major and minor ideas in this complex sentence: "I will go if you want me to." **Correlative conjunctions** are the conjunctions made of more than one word, such as *either/or,* and *neither/nor.*

interjection (interj.)	**shows emotion**	*Oh, wow, yes, no, well*

Interjections do not do anything special, such as join words, or modify words, or replace words. All they do is show emotion. If we say, "Wow, you look nice!" the word *wow* just shows happiness or excitement. The most common interjections are the words *yes* and *no.* Another very common interjection is the word *oh: Oh, yes,* I like interjections. Do you?

A Vocabulary Note

The word **preposition** contains two ancient Latin word pieces, or stems, that we see in many words, **pre** and **pos**. The stem **pre** means "before," and we see **pre** in words such as **predict** and **prepare**. The stem **pos** means "put," and we see **pos** in words such as **position** and **depose**. So the word **preposition** contains a picture: the **preposition** is the part that is "put before" the other words in the phrase. The word **conjunction** also contains stems which appear in many other words: **con** and **junct**. The stem **con** means "together," and the stem **junct** means "join." In the words **adverb** and **adjective**, we see the stem **ad**, which means "to," and the word **pronoun** contains the stem **pro**, which means "for" or sometimes "forward." The word **infinitive** contains the stems **in**, which means "not" in some words and "in" in others, and **fin**, which means "limit." Look up some of the following example words in your dictionary, and see if you can understand why they mean what they mean:

Stem	Meaning	Example Words
pre	before	predict, prepare, preliminary, preschool, preface, premonition
pos	put	position, depose, interpose, suppose, deposit, repose, appositive
con	together	conjunction, contact, connect, contiguous, contract, converge
junct	join	juncture, disjunction, injunction, adjunct, conjunction
ad	to	adjective, adverb, adherent, adjacent, adapt, admit
pro	for or forward	pronoun, propel, prophet, proponent, prominent, promote
in	not	infinite, indefinite, invalid, incomplete, ineligible, insane
in	in	inside, insert, inquest, inroad, inoculate, innards, innovate
fin	limit	infinitive, infinite, define, confine, finite, finitude, refine

Now, you know that the stem **ject** means "throw." In the word **object** we also see the stem **ob**, which means "toward" or "about." We see the stem **ob** in many words: *object, obstacle, obdurate, oblique, obloquy, objurgate,* and *obscure,* for example. Use your dictionary to look up the full etymology of the word **object,** and see if you can understand why we call objects *objects.* Then answer this question: *How are direct objects in sentences similar to objects on the ground?*

Review

Let's look again at what the eight kinds of words do. Study the parts of speech until you have their functions memorized. Make sure that you can remember some examples of each one.

noun
name of something   Mike, dog, tree, sound
The *boy* listened to the *music* of *Verdi.*

pronoun
replaces a noun   I, she, him, it, them
She and *I* saw *him* and *her* at the Museum of Modern Art.

adjective
modifies a noun or pronoun   red, tall, fast, good, the
Isaac Newton, *a famous* mathematician, discovered *the natural* law.

verb
an action or equals word   jumps, fell, is
I *lost* the Byron poem yesterday, but I *have* it now.

adverb
modifies a verb   quickly, slowly, well
The pianist played her Chopin solo *beautifully.*

preposition
shows relationship   in, on, beside, after
The government is *of* the people, *by* the people, and *for* the people.

conjunction	joins words	and, or, but

I saw the doctor, *and* she gave me some medicine.

interjection	shows emotion	Oh, wow, yes, no, well

Oh, yes, I always vote in the elections.

Examples

Now let's look at some sentences, and inspect the parts of speech in each one. We will use a little arrow, like this », to show what noun an adjective modifies, or to show what verb an adverb modifies.

    adj.   »   n.   v.   adj. » n.

1. **The   architect   designed   a   bridge.**
    subject   predicate

Notice that the noun *bridge* is a direct object of the action verb *designed*.

    n.   adv. »   v.   adj. » n.

2. **Michelangelo   carefully   painted   the   ceiling.**
    subject   predicate

Notice that the noun *ceiling* is a direct object of the action verb *painted*.

  interj. pron. conj. pron. v.   n.

3. **Yes,   you   and   I   are   friends.**
        subject   predicate

Notice that the noun *friends* is a subject complement of the linking verb *are*.

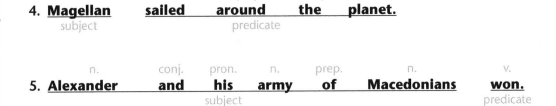

    n.   v.   prep.   adj. » n.

4. **Magellan   sailed   around   the   planet.**
    subject   predicate

    n.   conj. pron. n. prep.   n.   v.

5. **Alexander   and   his   army   of   Macedonians   won.**
        subject   predicate

Now, notice some very interesting things about the grammar of these sentences:

- The subject can be one word or many words.

- The predicate can be one word or many words.

- The main word of the subject is always a noun or pronoun.

- The main word of the predicate is always a verb.

- A sentence always contains a noun or pronoun and a verb.

Here are some more sentences. Study each one carefully, and imitate the five examples on the previous page by writing the abbreviation for the part of speech above each word, and by underlining the subject and predicate of each sentence. Identify any direct objects or subject complements you see.

1. **The   scientist   used   a   microscope.**

2. **Rembrandt   slowly   painted   the   canvas.**

3. **Yes,   he   and   she   were   members.**

4. **De Soto   floated   down   the   Mississippi.**

5. **Spartacus   and   his   force   of   gladiators   lost.**

Check your answers from the answer key on the next page.

A Vocabulary Note

The stem **micro** in the word **microscope** means "small." If you know that, then you know part of the meaning of many words. To illustrate this point, look at some of the words that contain the stem **micro**: *microline, microbe, microcephaly, microfiche, microbar, microcyte, microcosm, micrococcus, microfarad, microphyte, microlith, microgram, micrometer, Micronesia, micron, microspore, microwave, microsome, microsecond, microscope, micronucleus, microorganism, microphone, micrography, microgram, microseism, microtome.*

Look up some of the **micro** words that you do not know, and see what they mean.

Answer Key

    adj. » n.   v.   adj. » n.

1. **The   scientist   used   a   microscope.**
         subject   predicate

The noun *microscope* is a direct object.

          n.   adj. » v.   adj. » n.

2. **Rembrandt   slowly   painted   the   canvas.**
       subject   predicate

The noun *canvas* is a direct object.

   interj. pron. conj. pron.   v.   n.

3. **Yes,   he   and   she   were   members.**
             subject   predicate

The noun *members* is a subject complement.

        n.   v.   prep. adj. » n.

4. **De Soto   floated   down   the   Mississippi.**
     subject   predicate

        n.   conj.   pron.   n.   prep.   n.   v.

5. **Spartacus   and   his   force   of   gladiators   lost.**
                  subject   predicate

(I know, you want to know who Rembrandt, De Soto, and Spartacus were. Well, Rembrandt van Rijn was a Dutch master painter who was born in 1606 and died in 1669. Rembrandt did a self-portrait that is one of the most striking and penetrating in the history of art. Hernando De Soto was a courageous Spanish explorer, born about 1500, who is credited with discovering the Mississippi River, although the American Indians had actually discovered it long, long before any Europeans arrived in the New World. Spartacus was a proud Thracian slave in the Roman Empire who became a gladiator and who led a slave revolt against Rome. Spartacus and his men were annihilated in 71 B.C.)

One day, long, long ago, some human being uttered the first word. And language began. Over a period of time, human beings developed language, and more and more parts of speech were created, until there were eight. Use your common sense and imagination to guess what you think was probably the part of speech of the first words ever used. Think about it, and then write down your guess, and the reason you think it is probable.

The part of speech of the first word was _____.

I think this because: _____

_____

_____

_____

_____

_____

_____

_____

_____

_____

_____

_____

_____

_____

_____

_____

_____

_____

_____

5. Parts of the Sentence: Inside the Predicate

When we began this discussion of grammar, we saw that we express our ideas in language by using sentences made of two main parts, the subject and the predicate. In discussing the parts of speech, we saw that there are other parts of the sentence, such as the direct object and subject complement. Now it is time to review these terms and to elaborate on the ideas which we briefly touched on earlier. The complete subject may contain many words, but it will always include the simple subject, which is the noun or pronoun that the sentence is about. The **complete predicate** may also contain many words, but it will contain the **simple predicate**, which is the verb. So far this seems simple:

adj.	adj.	n.	v.	adv.	prep.	adj.	adj.	n.
Three	**blind**	**mice**	**ran**	**away**	**into**	**the**	**tall**	**grass.**

		subj.	pred.					

| complete subject | | | complete predicate | | | | | |

But actually, there are a few more details to explain, because as we have seen the predicate can contain several different kinds of special parts.

Sometimes, the predicate is very simple. A sentence might only have a noun and either an action or a linking verb. In fact, there is a famous sentence that illustrates this point, by the French philosopher Rene Descartes (1596–1650). Descartes was trying to prove that he positively knew that he existed, which sounds easy to do, but is actually quite difficult. Descartes said, "I think, therefore I am." In this sentence, we have a first person singular subject *I* followed by the action verb predicate *think,* and we later have the same pronoun again, followed by the same simple linking verb predicate *am.*

But what if Descartes had said, "I think thoughts, therefore I am a person"? How would we describe the nouns *thoughts* and *person,* since neither one is the subject of a verb?

Here is how: When an action verb clause shows the subject doing something **to something**, as in the sentence "The dog bit the mailman," we call the noun or pronoun that receives the action a **direct object**. *But* when a linking verb clause shows that the subject is **equal to or the same as** something else, as in the sentence "The dog is a poodle," we call the noun or pronoun that is linked to the subject a **subject complement**.

Direct Object: Achilles grabbed the **warrior**.

Subject Complement: Achilles was a **warrior**.

Notice that the only way to tell whether the second noun in these sentences is a direct object or a subject complement is to look at the *verb*. If a sentence contains an action verb, it might have a direct object, but if the sentence contains a linking verb, it might have a subject complement. This is a very advanced grammar idea, and it gives us deep insight into the way we form our own ideas.

Let's test your understanding. In the sentence, "Harlow Shapley, the great astronomer, saw the Andromeda galaxy," is *galaxy* a direct object or a subject complement? If your answer equals the seventeenth and eighteenth words in the preceding paragraph, you are right.

But what about this sentence: "Blaise Pascal was a French mathematician." Is the word *mathematician* a direct object or a subject complement? The answer is equal to the final words of the paragraph above that begins with the words, "Here is how."

Direct object or subject complement? It is all based on the *verb.* But notice the logic of these terms. The direct object IS directly affected by the verb, whereas the subject complement DOES complement (which means complete) our knowledge of the subject. Like so many terms in grammar, these terms are very easy to remember, because they are almost self-defining.

Now, are you ready to be trapped? Ok, try this sentence: "Odysseus gave the Cyclops a sore eye." The tricky question is, what is the word Cyclops? Is it the subject? The direct object? The subject complement? Well, the subject is the proper noun *Odysseus,* and the verb is a past tense action verb, *gave,* so we are looking for a direct object. But on close inspection, we see that the direct object is the common noun *eye.* The word *Cyclops* is what we call an **indirect object**. It is a noun or object pronoun that is located between the action verb and the direct object, and that is only indirectly affected by the action. There must be a direct object in order to have an indirect object.

And so we find that there are two primary parts of the sentence, the subject and the predicate, but that inside the predicate we might, or might not, find a direct object, an indirect object, or a subject complement. Let's review these terms. Think very carefully about what you have learned:

complete subject: what the sentence is about

simple subject: the noun or pronoun that the sentence is about

complete predicate: what we say about the subject

simple predicate: the verb

direct object: the noun or object pronoun that receives the action of the action verb

indirect object: the noun or object pronoun that is located between the action verb and the direct object, and that is indirectly affected by the action

subject complement: the noun, subject pronoun, or adjective that is linked to the subject by a linking verb

If you have carefully followed the discussion so far, you are ready for the last step. You got a glimpse of it in the definitions you just read. Notice that a direct object must be a noun or *object* pronoun: I watched the composer; I watched *him.* A subject complement, on the other hand, must be a noun, *subject* pronoun, or even an adjective. Remember that the subject pronouns are *I, you, he, she, it, we, you, they,* and the object pronouns are *me, you, him, her, it, us, you, them.* Direct objects, as their name suggests, always use object pronouns, but subject complements, as their name suggests, always use subject pronouns. Examples:

Direct object: I saw him.

Subject complement: It was he.

Direct object: It hit me.

Subject complement: It is I.

Now you finally know enough to understand why I insisted earlier that you memorize the subject and object pronouns. Sentences contain parts called subjects (subject of verb and

The 1940s: A Decade of Change · Student Grammar Study

subject complement), and sentences contain parts called objects (direct object, indirect object, and object of preposition). Those called subjects always use subject pronouns, and those called objects always use object pronouns. Period. A subject is a subject, and an object is an object.

If you do not understand your grammar well enough to know the parts of the sentence and the difference between subject and object pronouns, you will never be able to speak or write correctly. Guessing will not get you through. Your ear will not get you through. You must know, based on whether the verb is action or linking, whether you have a subject complement or a direct object, and choose your pronouns accordingly. Examples:

Matching Pronouns to the Parts of the Sentence:

Subject: *He and I* saw the dog.

Direct object: The dog chased *him and me.*

Subject complement: The visitors were *he and I.*

Object of preposition: The money was for *her and me.*

Indirect object: The chief gave *him and me* a broken arrow.

Everything: *He and I* saw *him and her,* but *she and I* gave *him and her* a prize, and it was *she and I* who laughed last.

Now, return to the top of this section, and read it through again, very carefully, until you feel confident about identifying the parts of the sentence and about choosing the correct pronouns for each part. Then choose the correct pronouns for the sentences below.

1. The postcard of Picasso's *Guernica* was sent to (he and I, him and me).

2. The debate was won by (she and I, her and me).

3. The discovery struck (she and I, her and me) with full force.

4. It was (her and me, she and I) who phoned.

5. (Him and me, He and I) arrived at the dock.

6. The professor gave (he and I, him and me) a book about Cervantes.

7. The present was for (she and I, her and me).

8. The conference audience applauded (she and I, her and me) loudly.

9. The winners of the competition were (him and me, he and I).

10. Bach's Brandenburg Concertos are the best music for (you and he, you and him).

Do you think that you made all of the choices correctly? Well, in every case, the correct answer was the second pair of pronouns. If you did not always select the second pair, then you need to go back and study the grammar of the sentence. Remember: the subject and object pronouns must be matched to the subject and object sentence parts. A direct object always uses object pronouns, and a subject complement always uses subject pronouns. The easy way to remember the pronoun rule is: A subject is a subject, and an object is an object.

6. Phrases: The Clever Teamwork

We all know what teams are. Five players work together on a basketball team, and each player has his or her own part in executing a well-practiced play. Cheerleaders work together to make a single pyramid, with each cheerleader standing on the shoulders of two cheerleaders below. Lawyers can work as a team to win a single case. Computer programmers work in teams to write programs, with each programmer specializing in writing a different part of the computer code. Doctors work in teams, with anesthesiologists working alongside surgeons.

Well, by inspecting our own ideas with grammar, we have discovered a remarkable thing. Sometimes, a whole group of words will team together to imitate a single part of speech! A team of words acting as a single part of speech is called a **phrase**. We learned a bit about **prepositional phrases** when we studied the parts of speech, but now we are ready to learn more. Here is a more complete definition of the phrase: *a phrase is a group of words that acts as a single part of speech, and that does not contain a subject and its predicate.* For example, notice that a prepositional phrase can behave as though it were an adverb, modifying a verb:

An ordinary adverb: The penguin sat **there**.

A phrase: The penguin sat **on the iceberg**.

In each case, the verb *sat* is being modified by something, but in the first example the verb is being modified by a simple adverb, *there*, whereas in the second example, the verb is being modified by **a group of words, *on the iceberg*, acting as a team to make an adverb.** That is what phrases are: word groups imitating other parts of speech. It is interesting, by the way, to note that our English word *phrase* comes from a very ancient Greek word, *phrazein*, which meant "to speak."

A prepositional phrase can also act as an adjective:

An ordinary adjective: The **top** book is a classic.

A phrase: The book **on the top** is a classic.

There are different kinds of phrases. Let's look at some other phrases, and see some of the interesting forms that phrases can take in sentences. Remember to notice that the phrase never contains both a sentence's subject and its predicate, and that a sentence can contain more than one phrase, or no phrase at all.

Phrases

Carmen, **my favorite opera**, is by the composer Bizet.

Not remembering names is my problem.

Birds fly **over the rainbow**.

I pledge allegiance **to the flag**.

The assault team climbed the north face **of Mount Everest**.

The problem's solution was very difficult, but we became determined. (no phrase!)

Magellan sailed **around the world**.

Newton loved **to study mathematics**.

The painting **on the museum's north wall** was painted **by the French painter, Monet**.

Now, go back and look very carefully at the phrases you just read, and see if you can tell which ones are like most of the others, and which ones are different. What do you notice as you look at the nine different phrases?

The first thing you probably notice is that most of the phrases are prepositional phrases. There are six of them. They begin with prepositions and end with nouns which are the objects of the prepositions.

What about the others? The phrase *my favorite opera* contains no preposition. Neither does *not remembering names.* The phrase *to study mathematics* sounds like a prepositional phrase at first, but then you realize that this is the infinitive verb *to study,* rather than the preposition *to.* What are these other kinds of phrases called, and how do they work?

Well, there are several important kinds of phrases to know about:

- The **prepositional phrase** is the one we already know about. It is always a modifier serving as a big adjective or adverb, and it always begins with a preposition. As we have seen, the phrase also contains a noun or pronoun which is an object of the preposition. Example: Magellan sailed **around the world**.

- An **appositive phrase** is an interrupting definition which is apposed (placed beside) the word it defines. Example: *Carmen,* **my favorite opera**, is by the composer Bizet.

- A **verbal phrase** is a phrase based on a verbal, which is a noun, adjective, or adverb made out of a verb. There are three kinds of verbals: **gerunds, participles,** and **infinitives**.

  - **A gerund** is a noun made out of a verb. Gerunds end in *-ing.* Example: **Not remembering names** is my problem. In this sentence, the gerund is the noun *remembering* which is used as the subject of the sentence. It is made out of the verb *to remember.*

  - **A participle** is an adjective made out of a verb. Participles end in various typical verb endings. Example: **Working quickly,** the painter splattered paint all over the canvas. In this sentence, the participle is the adjective *working,* which modifies the noun *painter.* This adjective is made out of the verb *to work.* Example: The **cracked** branch broke. The adjective *cracked* is made out of the verb *to crack.*

  - An **infinitive** is the infinitive form of the verb used as a noun, as an adjective, or as an adverb. Examples are: To work is a pleasure. (noun) The man to see is the Director. (adjective modifying the noun *man*) He lives to fish. (adverb modifying the verb *lives*)

What does this discussion of phrases show us? It shows us the incredible flexibility and creativity that our minds possess. This is especially true in the case of the verbals, which are possibly the most creative and imaginative element of the English language. In verbals, we see our brains leaping over barriers, extending the limits of what verbs can do, and forging new imaginative uses for words. Using verbals, we can communicate energetic and exciting ideas that would be impossible in any other way.

Conclusion

Now let's think carefully about all of the things that we have learned. We have learned a very important secret about the way we think and express our ideas about the world. The secret is that our ideas, which we sometimes call **sentences**, are only complete when they are made of two parts. These two parts are the **subject** that the sentence is about, and the **predicate** that says something about the subject. If we do not have both of these parts in our ideas, we will not have a complete thought, and we will not make any sense to anyone else. Other people have to know both of these parts in order to understand our ideas; they have to know what we are talking about, and they have to know what we are saying about it. When we extend this insight to all levels of communication—to the sentence, to the paragraph, to the essay—we have a deep understanding of the secret of clarity.

We have also learned an amazing secret about the thousands and thousands of words in our English language: incredible as it may seem, there are only eight basic kinds of words. We call these eight kinds of words the **parts of speech**. We have learned that each kind of word has a special purpose, a function, that it serves in a sentence. From these eight functions, language is made. Two of the parts of speech, the **noun** and the **verb**, are special, because they are in almost every sentence. The **subject** of a sentence usually has a **noun** (but it might have a **pronoun** instead to take the noun's place), and the **predicate** of the sentence always (yes, always) has a verb.

We have learned that parts of speech are also used as **parts of the sentence**. The **simple subject** is the noun or pronoun that the sentence is about. The **simple predicate** is the subject's verb. The **direct object** is a noun or pronoun that receives the action of the action verb, and the **subject complement** is the noun or pronoun linked to the subject, by the linking verb. The **indirect object** is the noun or object pronoun that is located between the action verb and the direct object, and that is indirectly affected by the action.

We have learned that our minds are clever enough to collect little groups of words together into **phrases** that imitate other parts of speech, and we have seen examples of phrases acting as adverbs, as adjectives, and even as nouns. We have seen **prepositional phrases** that are used as modifiers, **appositive phrases** that are interrupting definitions, and three different kinds of **verbal phrases**, in which verbs are changed into other parts of speech. **Gerund phrases** use -*ing* verbs as nouns. **Participial phrases** use verbs as adjectives. And **infinitive phrases** use verbs as nouns, adjectives or adverbs.

Finally, **verbs** have taught us a very important secret about ideas. Since there are two kinds of verbs, the **action** kind and the **equals** or **linking** kind, this means that there are two main kinds of ideas. We can either say that the **subject is doing something**, or we can say that the **subject is something**. For example, we can use an action verb and say, "The reader of this book saw a very good student." But if we use an equals verb, we can say something even better: "The reader of this book is a very good student."

Copyright © Kendall Hunt Publishing Company

adj.	n.	prep.	adj.	n.	v.	adj.	adv.	adj.	n.
The	**reader**	**of**	**this**	**book**	**is**	**a**	**very**	**good**	**student.**

simple subj.   prep. phrase   simple pred.   subject complement

——————————————————————   ——————————————————————

complete subject   complete predicate

———

a one-clause sentence

Now, that is a good, two-part, linking verb idea. As you see, grammar is a fascinating way to think about our own thinking. Using grammar, we can examine our thoughts, and we can see how we have made them. If we did not have grammar, we would never really be able to understand how powerful our minds are. But after this short introduction to grammar, you have begun to understand how powerfully your mind makes ideas out of language. As you learn more and more about grammar in the future, you will gain a greater insight into how wonderful it is to be a human being, an idea-maker. I hope that you will always look forward to the wonderful study of grammar. It is truly a way of inspecting our own ideas.